CALLED
TO
REBUILD

BOB EMERY

CALLED TO REBUILD

THE RESTORATION *of the* HOUSE *of* GOD

Pleasant Word
A Division of WINEPRESS PUBLISHING

Cover design taken from Gustave Dore's "The Rebuilding of the Temple."

Pleasant Word (a division of WinePress Publishing, PO Box 428, Enumclaw, WA 98022) functions only as book publisher. As such, the ultimate design, content, editorial accuracy, and views expressed or implied in this work are those of the author.

Published by: BenchPress Publishing, P.O. Box 5846, Charlottesville, VA 22905, USA. Website: www.therevelation.com.

Unless otherwise noted, all Scriptures are taken from the New American Standard Bible, © 1960, 1963, 1968, 1971, 1972, 1973, 1975, 1977 by The Lockman Foundation. Used by permission.

ISBN 13: 978-1-4141-0951-0
ISBN 10: 1-4141-0951-2
Library of Congress Catalog Card Number: 2007922413

To all who have a heart to rebuild the house of God on its original foundation—which is Jesus Christ.

TABLE OF CONTENTS

ACKNOWLEDGEMENTS

This book was the result of a series of messages given on the book of Ezra to a group of believers meeting together in a home fellowship in Charlottesville, Virginia. Though our study concentrated on the book of Ezra, in order for us to see the complete picture of what God did during this restoration period covering the last 100 years of history documented in the Old Testament, it was also necessary to draw from the book of Nehemiah, and from the prophets Haggai, Zecharia, and Malachi. Together, all of these books give us the full picture of what God was able to accomplish and what he had to say to the remnant that was called to rebuild the temple, restore the wall, and reinhabit the city of Jerusalem that had been laid waste by the Babylonians. I'd like to thank them for being a willing audience.

A significant portion of what you will be reading here is a compilation of the fruit others' labors. I feel extremely fortunate to have been influenced by men whom I consider to be among the finest Christ-centered Bible teachers and ministers of the

Word today. All of these men have had significant experience outside of the traditional practice of denominational Christianity that has given them a unique perspective on this subject. I'd like to especially thank Ed Miller from Rhode Island, one of the most Christ-centered Bible teachers that I know. For more than 40 years Ed has been a devoted student of the Scriptures. I rejoice for all the times that he has emerged from his vast library and studies to edify and encourage the Lord's people by giving them a fresh vision of Christ. In one series of messages, Ed gave a lengthy study on the book of Ezra that was recorded on 18 audio tapes. I listened to all of those tapes and gleaned a great deal of insight and information that has been incorporated into this book. I'd also like to acknowledge Stephen Kaung, who was a co-worker with Watchman Nee in China. Stephen is personally responsible for translating most of brother Nee's writings into English. I've always held Stephen in the highest regard as being one of the best Bible teachers I have ever known. Stephen has spoken and written extensively on the theme found in Ezra, namely, the rebuilding the house of God, and has contributed greatly to my understanding of the subject. I'd also like to convey my appreciation to Dana Congdon, a friend and Bible teacher from New York, whose messages have also contributed to the content of this book.

I want to express a special thanks to Gene Edwards, whom God used as a "Cyrus" in my life to challenge me, along with a group of other young Christians nearly 40 years ago, to follow the example of the remnant and rise up to rebuild the house of God upon its original foundation. I owe a great debt to Gene for the revelation of Christ and the church that I received through his ministry. Finally, I'd like to convey my deepest gratitude to that band of brothers and sisters from Isla Vista, California, who responded to God's call and embarked on a quest to see the church as alive and vibrant as it was in the first century become a reality once again. Together with them, I had the greatest privilege to experience much of what is written in this book.

Cyrus releases the Jews
"Going Home"
By
Julius Schnorr von Carolsfeld
1851-60

INTRODUCTION

"The counsel of the Lord stands forever, the plans of his heart from generation to generation."

(Ps. 33:11)

"Now to Him who is able to do far more abundantly beyond all that we ask or think, according to the power that works within us, to Him be the glory in the church and in Christ Jesus to all generations forever and ever. Amen."

(Eph. 3:20-21)

"Then I turned to see the voice that was speaking with me. And having turned I saw seven golden lampstands and in the middle of the lampstands I saw one like the Son of Man...As for the mystery of the seven stars which you saw in My right hand, and the seven golden lampstands; the seven stars are the angels of the seven churches, and the seven lampstands are the seven churches."

(Rev. 1:12, 13, 20)

WHY THIS BOOK?

In the fall of 2005 I attended a retreat that focused on the subject of the house church movement in America. It wasn't the first house church conference I've attended or participated in. I've been interested and involved in house church and participatory, interactive meetings with groups of believers in homes for the past 38 years.

About the same time a new book by George Barna was released called *Revolution*. Barna heads up a research firm in California called The Barna Group, and for 24 years has done research for churches, Christian organizations, and secular organizations (including The Billy Graham Evangelistic Association, Focus on the Family, and countless others). In his book Barna identifies some of the growing trends within the professed church of America. It seems to confirm a growing movement among American Christians, alarming to some and liberating to others, regarding the practice of "church." According to Barna's predictions, which are based on years of surveys and interviews, by the year 2025 there will be a 30% decrease in the number of Christians attending traditional church.

Among those who would find this information alarming are those people committed to the existing system for practicing "church," and particularly pastors, who have no other job skills and are dependent on maintaining their congregations in tact for fear of losing their support base.

But to a smaller group of Christians in America this information is liberating and affirming. People who fall into this category already think that there is something wrong with the religious system and have gone on to find more meaning, purpose, and significant relationships in smaller groups characterized by interaction, joint participation, praying together, and sharing their needs and lives. Barna identifies more than 20 million of these "revolutionaries" among American Christians and their numbers are growing.

Here is how he describes them:

What makes Revolutionaries so startling is that they are confidently returning to a first-century lifestyle based on faith, goodness, love, generosity, kindness, simplicity, and other values deemed "quaint" by today's frenetic and morally untethered standards. This is not the defeatist retreat of an underachieving, low-capacity mass of people. It is an intelligent and intentional embrace of a way of life that is the only viable antidote to the untenable moral standards, dysfunctional relationships, material excess, abusive power, and unfortunate misapplication of talent and knowledge that pass for life in America these days. Many Revolutionaries have tested the alternatives and found them woefully inadequate. Now, like children who sheepishly realize that Mama was right all along, they have gratefully and humbly accepted the opportunity to do what is right, simply because it is right, even if it is not original or culturally hip...

As we journey together, I want to show you what our research has uncovered regarding a growing sub-nation of people, already well over 20 million strong, who are what we call Revolutionaries.

What "established systems" are they seeking to "overthrow or repudiate" and "thoroughly replace," in Webster's words?

They have no use for churches that play religious games, whether those games are worship services that drone on without the presence of God or ministry programs that bear no spiritual fruit. Revolutionaries eschew ministries that compromise or soft sell our sinful nature to expand organizational turf. They refuse to follow people in ministry leadership positions who cast a personal vision rather than God's, who seek popularity rather than the proclamation of truth in their public statements, or who are more concerned about their own legacy than that of Jesus Christ. They refuse to donate one more dollar to man-made monuments that mark their own achievements and guarantee their place in history. They are unimpressed by accredited degrees and endowed chairs in Christian colleges and seminaries that produce young people incapable of defending the Bible or unwilling to devote their lives to serving others. And Revolutionaries are embarrassed by language that promises Christian love and holiness but turns out to be all sizzle and no substance.

In fact, many Revolutionaries have been active in good churches that have biblical preaching, people coming to Christ and being baptized, a full roster of interesting classes and programs, and a congregation packed with nice people. There is nothing overtly wrong with anything taking place at some churches. But Revolutionaries innately realize that it is just not enough to go with the flow. The experience provided through their church, although better than average, still seems flat. They are seeking a faith experience that is more robust and awe inspiring, a spiritual journey that prioritizes transformation at every turn, something worthy of the Creator whom their faith reflects. They are seeking the spark provided by a commitment to a true revolution in thinking, behavior, and experience, where settling for what is merely good and above average is defeat.

(Revolution, pages 12-15)

Here is a sample of statistics, taken from a long list, that Barna has gained from his research concerning the condition of the 77 million American adults who are churched, born-again Christians. These are real people. Put a face on them. Most likely they include people you know. They could even be referring to you!

Regarding Worship...

- The biweekly attendance at worship services is, by believers' own admission, generally the only time they worship God.
- Eight out of every ten believers do not feel they have entered into the presence of God, or experienced a connection with Him, during the worship service.
- Half of all believers say they do not feel they have entered into the presence of God or experienced a genuine connection with Him during the past year.

Regarding Faith-Based Conversations...

- The typical churched believer will die without leading a single person to a lifesaving knowledge of and relationship with Jesus Christ.
- At any given time, a majority of believers do not have a specific person in mind for whom they are praying in hope that the person will be saved.

Regarding Intentional Spiritual Growth...

- Only 9 percent of all born-again adults have a biblical worldview—meaning that less than one out of every ten Christians age eighteen or older believes that absolute moral truth exists, believes that such truth is contained in the Bible, and possesses a handful of core beliefs that reflect such truth. Those beliefs include a certainty that the Bible is accurate in its teachings; Jesus lived a sinless life on earth; Satan is real, not symbolic; all believers are responsible for sharing their faith in Christ with others; the only means to salvation is through God's grace; and God is the all-knowing and all-powerful creator of the universe who still rules it today.

Regarding Resource Investment...

- Churched Christians give away an average of about 3 percent of their income in a typical year—and feel pleased at their "sacrificial" generosity.
- Fewer than one out of every ten churched Christians donates at least 10 percent of their incomes to churches and other nonprofit organizations.
- Most believers are unable to identify anything specific they have ever donated money to that they would describe as producing life-changing outcomes.

Regarding Family Faith...

- The likelihood of a married couple who are born-again churchgoers getting divorced is the same as couples who are not disciples of Jesus. (Revolution, pages 31-35)

Barna identifies four main categories of Christians: those who are seeking relevance and meaning 1) from the traditional church structure, 2) through some form of house church experience, 3) through an emphasis on family as the smallest unit for the church, and 4) through exploring the universes of "cyber-church." Among these, the house church and the "cyber-church" are the fastest growing.

With people going in so many directions, this state of affairs reminds me of the last verse in the book of Judges where it says, *"In those days there was no King in Israel; everyone did what was right in his own eyes."* Coming off this house church conference and reading Barna's book, I was motivated to go back to one of my favorite books in the Old Testament—the book of Ezra—to rekindle afresh in my heart what God is after and see how this book might apply to the situation we find ourselves in today.

It is comforting to know that God didn't leave his people in the state they were in at the close of the book of Judges. He was moving forward. He raised up David, his appointed King, established the kingdom, and through Solomon built the temple and established a permanent place of worship in Jerusalem.

God's purpose has not changed. In the Old Testament, David and the temple were only pictures pointing to what God would do when Christ, the eternal King, would come. His plan has always been to establish Jesus Christ as the King of Kings and Lord of Lords, to bring his heavenly reign to earth, and to build his church, which is the true temple and his eternal dwelling place. We see glimpses of the glory of the first century church on the pages of the New Testament. We can read about various groups throughout history that left the religious system of their day and returned to the simplicity of knowing Christ together and became a testimony to their generation. Clearly, with the parallels we see regarding the spiritual condition of the church today and those at the time of Ezra when the temple lay in waste and ruin, what better book would there be to study than the book of Ezra, and the related books of Nehemiah, Haggai, Zechariah, and Malachi? The message in these books to a people in quest of rebuilding the Lord's house, which is his church, is just as applicable now as it was then. In fact, in the words of Paul, *"Now all these things happened to them* (Moses, and the people in the Old Testament) *as examples and*

> *David and the temple were only pictures pointing to what God would do when Christ, the eternal King, would come. His plan has always been to establish Jesus Christ as the King of Kings and Lord of Lords, to bring his heavenly reign to earth, and to build his church, which is the true temple and his eternal dwelling place.*

they were written for our instruction, upon whom the ends of the ages have come" (1 Corinthians 10:11).

WHERE IS GOD IN ALL OF THIS WE'RE SEEING TODAY?

Rather than reacting with alarm to the current church trends, I welcome this information as evidence that God is stirring in the hearts of men and women today to seek a more relevant, biblical experience of the church. My hope and prayer is that across this country, thousands of groups of seeking ones within the greater body of Christ will be raised up and become lampstands that will truly lift up and exalt the Lord Jesus Christ according to God's original design.

Certainly this is not the first time in history that reformers or revolutionaries have attempted to return to a purer, more primitive expression of the church. Martin Luther and the other leading reformers saw the condition of the Roman Catholic Church in their day and likened it to "Babylon." They called on people to come out and separate themselves from a system that they thought had become too corrupt. This led to the birth of the Protestant Reformation.

Following the reformers were the Anabaptists and other groups scholars have lumped together as "stepchildren of the reformers." They thought that Luther, Calvin, Zwingli, and others didn't go far enough in returning to a biblical model of the church. Consequently, they broke away from the state church in pursuit of an even purer, simpler practice of knowing Christ together.

Throughout history the battle over the church being expressed on this earth has raged. Is the church expressing the life of its invisible, heavenly Head, or has the fire of first love gone out and has it succumbed to the forces of institutionalism, ritual, complacency, and spiritual death? In every generation God's call has gone out to those who were willing to return to the Word of God, to follow the leading of his Spirit, and to establish a testimony of the church in keeping with its original design, that Christ would be lifted up, glorified, and come to have first place in all things.

> *In every generation God's call has gone out to those who were willing to return to the Word of God, to follow the leading of his Spirit, and to establish a testimony of the church in keeping with its original design, that Christ would be lifted up, glorified, and come to have first place in all things.*

As we study the Scriptures, we can see that even in the first century, in the decade leading up to the fall of Jerusalem in A.D. 70, the church had already lapsed into a period of decline. In the last letters of the apostles—I, II Timothy, I, II Peter, I, II, III John, Jude, Hebrews, and Revelation, we find many of the problems that led to this apostasy. False doctrine, legalism, worldly philosophies, and a return to Jewish nationalism had all entered into the church and corrupted a "simplicity and purity of devotion to Christ."

In the first three chapters of the book of Revelation nearly all of the seven churches had problems and to each one the Spirit issued a call to those who would overcome.

One of those churches was the church in Ephesus. Paul wrote his letter to the Ephesians in A.D. 62 from a Roman prison when the church was in its prime. The loftiness of the revelation contained in the Ephesian letter was one of the high-water marks of all first-century Christian writing. But with the passing of only about five years, when John wrote the book of Revelation (approximately A.D. 67), the church in Ephesus had left its first love and was warned that unless it repent, its lampstand would be removed. The believers in that city were still doing a lot of good work and enduring persecution. They knew correct doctrine and hated things that the Lord hated, but in spite of all their activity, John's inspired letter did not call them simply to make some minor adjustments. Because they had lost their first love, which was Christ, they were dangerously close to having their lampstand (their testimony) removed by the Lord altogether! This disastrous slide took place in only five years!

In order to return to a practice of the church consistent with what we read about in the New Testament, we need light from the Lord and a moving of his Spirit. In the late 1960s and early 1970s there was a move of God in America where the Spirit of God brought revival. During that revival the Scriptures were opened to many Christian leaders throughout the country. They preached from that light they were given resulting in what has come to be known as the Jesus Movement, which spread from one coast of this land to the other.

During those years there were many Christian experiences that we read about in the New Testament that were recovered and experienced once again in a fresh and living way. Two examples were the practice of baptism and taking the Lord's Supper. For many Christians this was a time when the blinders came off and the lights came on. Where in the New Testament did it ever say that in order to be baptized it required that it be done inside a building, in a small tank of water, and officiated by an ordained pastor with a seminary degree? Yet that was the practice of virtually every Christian in America prior to the Jesus movement. Leading up to that move of the Spirit, no one had even questioned that baptism could be done in any other way, or, God forbid, by anyone other than a member of the professional clergy.

Likewise, there was the practice of taking the Lord's Supper. Where in the New Testament does it say that we can only partake of the Lord's Supper inside a building with a cross on the top of it and only when its officiated by an ordained pastor or clergyman? And where on earth did we ever get the notion that the bread and the wine, taken with a meal along with other believers in someone's home (like we read about in the New Testament) is out of date and has been superseded by a superior model of partaking of a small, tasteless wafer and a thimble-sized portion of grape juice while sitting on a hard bench in a warehouse-sized room full of people, most of whom you don't know?

The generation of the late 1960s and early 1970s witnessed the almost spontaneous outbreak of baptisms (by laymen) in the ocean, in rivers, in lakes, and in swimming pools throughout the country. The Lord's Supper moved out of church buildings and into homes. The taboo that this was an event so holy that it could only be administered by a holy man (a pastor or clergyman) inside a holy place (a church building) was dashed. Common, ordinary Christians began reclaiming their God-given rights and privileges as New Testament believers, taking back those things that had been hoarded by the religious class.

During the late 1960s and the early 1970s common, ordinary Christians began reclaiming their God-given rights and privileges as New Testament believers, taking back those things that had been hoarded by the religious class.

God shed light from his Word, and people responded. Many "revolutionaries" of that generation began to experience a return to a practice of the church more consistent with what we read in the pages of the New Testament. Accompanying that fresh move of the Spirit was an overwhelming sense of joy and freedom. Something that was lost was being recovered.

THE BOOKS CONCERNING THE REMNANT— A ROADMAP TO RECOVERY

During those years of the Jesus Movement as God breathed on the Scriptures bringing many truths from the New Testament to light, the way people thought about "church" began to change. Thousands of people were impacted and still today, look back to those days as the most spiritually significant days of their lives. What they experienced of the moving of the Spirit has characterized similar movements across the earth where God has chosen to breathe new life, bring revival, and give his people a taste of what it was like in the first century church. But in addition to light from the New Testament, we have the Old Testament to instruct us as well.

The Old Testament was not written for us only to know as history. As God breathes upon those ancient texts we can learn the spiritual lessons from the experience of those who went before us and apply those lessons today. With God's help and revelation, we will come to understand the Old Testament as the New Testament, only in picture form, and this will become a roadmap leading to recovery. The lessons that we can learn from the story of the remnant should impact our daily living, our priorities, our understanding of the church, and our practice of the Christian life, both individually and corporately.

The book of Ezra is a book about the rebuilding of the temple in Jerusalem. The temple had been laid waste and God's people taken captive into a foreign land. But God's call was to bring the people back from their captivity, back to his original purpose, and rebuild the temple on its original foundation. The story continues in the book of Nehemiah with the rebuilding of the wall and the restoration of the city.

Today the church is the temple of God. The church has gone astray from its intended purpose of being a brightly shining lampstand, holding up Christ as the light of the world in this age of darkness. God wants to restore. God wants to rebuild. He will not compromise his standards. He has given us the Scriptures, and in particular, these precious books concerning the remnant, to shine light on the ancient pathway by which he will bring this about.

As we look at the book of Ezra and these other books, I must point out that our need is not just for more knowledge—theological or historical. Our need is for light from the Lord and revelation coming from his Spirit that will enable us to recover old, but discarded truths, and allow the Spirit to blow in a fresh way in our midst so that God will have a testimony for himself that will bring honor and glory to his Son.

For Whom Is This Book Written?

Hopefully everyone who reads this book will gain some new insights and understanding of the books of Ezra, Nehemiah, Haggai, Zechariah, and Malachi. Like most all of the books in the Bible, these books can be read, taught, or studied from the standpoint of "What does it mean to me, the individual Christian?" "What lessons can I, as an individual Christian, take from these books and apply to my life?"

However, this book was not primarily written to individual Christians seeking their own personal edification. This book was written for the adventurous and the daring—for those "groups" of revolutionaries that Barna describes whom God has brought together, who no longer have a stomach for a boring, predictable, lackluster Christian or church experience, but who are seeking more of a God-intended practice of New Testament church life. For you, I hope that this book will provide some guidance and instruction that will challenge you and give you a preview of what to expect as you embark on this quest.

When we look at this matter of rebuilding the ruined temple, it must be acknowledged that this was a corporate endeavor. It was not a task for any one individual. The books of Ezra and Nehemiah portray a company of people, a remnant that went back to the temple site to rebuild. So as you read the material presented in this book, keep in mind that I am presenting the message it contains as I believe it was intended to be presented: as if I were addressing a corporate group of people who have the heart to start all over again and rebuild the house of God on its original foundations.

To get the most out of this book, I highly recommend that you go back to the original sources of Ezra, Nehemiah, Haggai, Zechariah, and Malachi and read them for yourself. With these books fresh in your mind, much of the commentary in *Called to Rebuild* will naturally fall into place and be more easily understood.

TIMELINE

The timeline below is a concise overview of the history of God's dealing with his people leading up to and including the period of Ezra and Nehemiah and the remnant's return. It is important to note that the rebuilding of the temple (along with the restoration of the wall and the city), spanned a period of more than 100 years. From this overview we can see that when God restored his house in the Old Testament the work was very deliberate; it had in view a full restoration, and it did take some time. The same principles still apply today as we consider God's work in restoring the church to what he has always intended for it to be.

Date (B.C.) Event

1451	Israel crossed the Jordan and entered the Promised Land.
1085	King David was born.

1048	David was made king over all Israel.
1015	Solomon became king.
1012	The foundation of the temple was laid.
1006	The temple was dedicated to God.
975	King Solomon died.
606	Nebuchadnezzar's reign in Babylon began.
605	Jeremiah prophesied concerning the 70-year captivity.
605	Nebuchadnezzar first attacked Jerusalem. The sacred vessels from the temple were carried away.
586	The reign of Zedekiah, the last in the line of Israel's Kings, ended. Nebuchadnezzar launched his final siege against Jerusalem.
536	This was the first year of Cyrus' reign when he issued the decree for all those who wanted to return to Jerusalem to rebuild the temple.
536	The remnant returned with Zerubbabel and Jeshua to begin rebuilding the temple. Work began on the altar and foundation.
534	The work came to a stop because of opposition by the Samaritans.
522	The building was ordered to stop by royal decree.
521	Haggai and Zechariah began to prophesy.
520	The building resumed.
516	The temple was finished and dedicated.
474	This was the period in which the story of Esther took place.
458	Ezra was commissioned to return to Jerusalem.
457	The year in which Ezra chapters seven through ten took place.

444	Nehemiah was commissioned and the wall was rebuilt in 52 days.
432 (?)	Malachi prophesied during this time.
415	The book of Nehemiah came to a close.

Chapter One

A Brief Historical Background
Pre-Captivity

The books of Ezra and Nehemiah tell us the story of the remnant that returned from captivity in Babylon to rebuild Solomon's temple, the wall around Jerusalem, and the city of Jerusalem itself, which had been completely destroyed by King Nebuchadnezzar of Babylon.

Before jumping right into that story, I'd like to set the stage by reviewing some of the history leading up to the remnant's return.

Nearly 1,500 years before the birth of Christ, God sent his servant Moses to deliver his people from slavery in Egypt. He brought them through the wilderness to the land of Canaan, which God had given them to be their inheritance. From the time the people entered the land of Canaan until David became king over all Israel was a period of about 400 years. This was known as the period of the Judges.

The book of Judges can be characterized as a period of both revival and defeat. When God's people were oppressed by the

enemies that they failed to drive out of the land, they would cry
for help and God would deliver them by raising up a judge and
bring revival. But revival and peace was short-lived and before
long the people once again rebelled and the cycle repeated itself
of their crying out to God, God having mercy one more time,
and delivering them. God raised up thirteen judges during this
period, none of whom judged all of Israel at any one time.

The book of Judges ends with the verse that says, *"And at
that time there was no King in Israel and everyone did what was
right in his own eyes."* From that point Israel's history picks up
again in the book of I Samuel, where we read about how God
raised up Samuel, the priest. The word of God was rare in those
days but God began speaking once again to Samuel. The people
wanted to have a king for themselves like the other nations
around them so they chose Saul. In doing so, they rejected God
himself as their king. Saul reigned in Israel for 40 years. With
his death, David, the king chosen by God, came to the throne
and ruled over Israel for another 40 years. Following David,
Solomon became king.

With Solomon's ascension to the throne the temple was
built and dedicated. This was the pinnacle, the highest point
for the people of Israel in all the Old Testament. God had his
people in the land enjoying their inheritance. They had a king
reigning over them who was known for his great wealth and
wisdom. The people were united. They had the most beautiful,
glorious temple ever built. Kings and queens and people would
come from all over the earth just to see and admire it. God's
glory had come down from heaven and filled the temple and
he was living in their midst.

But that zenith did not last for long. Gradually Solomon
began to turn away from God. He married many foreign wives
and began to backslide. When he died a number of kings

succeeded him. Some were good. Others were very bad. But generally speaking, the state of the nation and of the kingdom was on a slide downward.

From the time of Saul until the end of the reign of the last king of Israel, Zedekiah, was another period of about 500 years. Nebuchadnezzar, Babylon's greatest king, began his reign in 606 B.C. He repeatedly invaded Judah and Jerusalem. Finally, in 588 B.C. he launched his final raid on Jerusalem that ended in 586. Many Israelites were killed. The rest were taken away to Babylon. This was known as the Babylonian captivity.

About the time that Nebuchadnezzar came to power, God raised up the prophet Jeremiah. Jeremiah prophesied concerning the captivity, proclaiming that it would last for a period of 70 years:

> "Therefore thus says the Lord of hosts, 'Because you have not obeyed My words, behold, I will send and take all the families of the north,' declares the Lord, 'and I will send to Nebuchadnezzar King of Babylon, My servant, and will bring them against this land and against its inhabitants and against all these nations round about; and I will utterly destroy them and make them a horror and a hissing, and an everlasting desolation. Moreover, I will take from them the voice of joy and the voice of gladness, the voice of the bridegroom and the voice of the bride, the sound of the millstones and the light of the lamp. This whole land will be desolation and a horror, and these nations will serve the king of Babylon seventy years."
>
> (Jeremiah 25:8-11)

He went on to say that at the end of those 70 years, God would judge Babylon. Both of these prophesies were fulfilled precisely 70 years later in 536 B.C., when King Cyrus of Persia defeated the Babylonians and a remnant from among the Jews returned from their captivity in Babylon to rebuild the temple. This is the story recorded in the book of Ezra.

Ezra, the author of the book bearing his name, was no small figure among Old Testament characters. He was purportedly the one who collected all the books of the Old Testament and put them together in one book. He is also credited with writing I and II Chronicles (the books coming just before the book of Ezra in the Bible), portions of Nehemiah, and even the book of Esther. We can see the continuity between II Chronicles and the book of Ezra by comparing the last two verses of the one book with the first two verses of the other. They are the same. So Ezra wrote I and II Chronicles, Ezra, portions of Nehemiah, Esther, and put together the whole Old Testament. He was a man of remarkable stature in the Old Testament and greatly used by God. It was Ezra's pen in II Chronicles 36:11-21 that recorded the sad condition of God's people and the final scene before their deportation to Babylon:

> *Zedekiah was twenty-one years old when he became king, and he reigned eleven years in Jerusalem. He did evil in the sight of the Lord his God; he did not humble himself before Jeremiah the prophet who spoke for the Lord. He also rebelled against King Nebuchadnezzar who had made him swear allegiance by God. But he stiffened his neck and hardened his heart against turning to the Lord God of Israel. Furthermore, all the officials of the priests and the people were very unfaithful following all the abominations of the nations; and they defiled the house of the Lord which He had sanctified in Jerusalem. The Lord, the God of their fathers, sent word to them again and again by His messengers, because He had compassion on His people and on His dwelling place; but they continually mocked the messengers of God, despised His words and scoffed at His prophets, until*

the wrath of the Lord arose against His people, until there was no remedy. Therefore he brought up against them the king of the Chaldeans who slew their young men with the sword in the house of their sanctuary, and had no compassion on young man or virgin, old man or infirm; He gave them all into his hand. All the articles of the house of God, great and small, and the treasures of the house of the Lord, and the treasures of the king and of his officials, he brought them all to Babylon. Then they burned the house of God and broke down the wall of Jerusalem, and burned all its fortified buildings with fire and destroyed all its valuable articles. Those who had escaped from the sword he carried away to Babylon and they were servants to him and to his sons until the rule of the kingdom of Persia, to fulfill the word of the Lord by the mouth of Jeremiah until the land had enjoyed its Sabbaths. All the days of its desolation it kept Sabbath until seventy years were complete.

From this passage we learn that Israel's last king, Zedekiah, was evil, proud, rebellious, inflexible, and hard-hearted (verses 12, 13). The priests and the people were unfaithful (verse 14). The Lord had sent word to them again and again by his messengers, the prophets, because he had compassion on them but they would not listen (verse 15). Finally they came to the point where God saw no remedy for them (verse 16). As a result, God gave them into Nebuchadnezzar's hand. He slaughtered many of the Israelites and took the rest captive and brought them, along with the articles of the house of God, to Babylon (verses 17-18). The house of God was burned and the wall around Jerusalem torn down (verse 19). This fulfilled the word of the Lord to Jeremiah (verse 21).

This passage states that the people were unfaithful and would not listen, so God had no alternative but to bring judgment against them. But why did the Lord say they would be in captivity for 70 years? Why not 50 years? Why not 100 years? Was there any one sin that stood out above all others that caused God to discipline his people by bringing them into captivity for 70 years?

But why did the Lord say they would be in captivity for 70 years? Why not 50 years? Why not 100 years? Was there any one sin that stood out above all others that caused God to discipline his people by bringing them into captivity for 70 years?

Was it idolatry? Immorality? Unholy alliances? Rebellion? Worldliness? Materialism? The answer could be "yes" to all of these questions. But was there one root sin that was at the core of what caused them to be led away into captivity? Since the Old Testament was written for our instruction, if we can discover what that was, we will have learned a great lesson that should serve as a compass to guide us in our own spiritual journeys.

Chapter Two

SO THAT'S HOW WE GOT HERE!
THE ROOT CAUSE OF THE CAPTIVITY

"For thus says the Lord, 'When seventy years have been completed for Babylon, I will visit you and fulfill My good word to you, to bring you back to this place. For I know the plans that I have for you,' declares the Lord, 'plans for welfare and not for calamity to give you a future and a hope.'"

(Jer. 29: 10, 11)

In the Old Testament God gave his people the land of Canaan as their inheritance. It was a rich land, flowing with milk and honey. In the words of Moses, it was

"...a good land, a land of brooks of water, of fountains and springs, that flow out of valleys and hills; a land of wheat and barley, of vines and fig trees and pomegranates, a land of olive oil and honey; a land in which you will eat bread without scarcity, in which you will lack nothing; a land whose stones are iron and out of whose hills you can dig copper. When you have eaten and

are full, then you shall bless the Lord your God for the good land which He has given you."

(Deut. 8: 7-10)

In the New Testament, the land is never mentioned as part of a Christian's inheritance. The Old Testament gave us the picture. For Israel it was a physical inheritance. God purposed to plant his people in the land he had chosen for their inheritance and for them to draw

> *Our inheritance is far greater than anything an Old Testament believer could ever have imagined. Our inheritance is Christ.*

everything they needed from that land. But for the Christian, ours is a spiritual inheritance. Our inheritance is far greater than anything an Old Testament believer could ever have imagined. Our inheritance is Christ (Eph. 1:11). In him, we have been blessed with every spiritual blessing (Eph. 1:3). The symbolism of the rich land with its springs, wheat, barley, oil, honey, iron, and so forth, corresponds to different aspects of the vast resources and bounty we have in Christ. For instance, the brooks, fountains, and springs speak of Christ as our living water; the olive oil symbolizes Christ as the Holy Spirit indwelling and anointing us; the honey represents the sweetness of Christ; while the iron denotes the strength of Christ, and so on.

When you put your faith in Christ, he came into you by his Spirit and you were born again. You received new life. That life is God, in Christ, in you. Now Christ is in you. But that's only half the story. The other half of the story is that God also put you *in Christ* (I Cor. 1:30). He planted us in our inheritance (Christ) in whom are all the spiritual resources and blessings we will ever need.

So, God brought his people into the land of Canaan through the leadership of his servant Joshua. Joshua divided up the land among the twelve tribes. Each tribe began to discover the riches allotted to them in the portion of the land they were given. But over time, due to their unfaithfulness, they lost the land. God eventually disciplined his people by sending *his servant*, Nebuchadnezzar, King of Babylon, to take them away into captivity for 70 years.

How can we apply this analogy to our situation today? When we begin our Christian lives we receive the whole land (Christ) within us—in our spirits. He is ours. We begin to enjoy him and his rich blessings. But over time, due to our unfaithfulness, we can begin to lose the experience of drawing our strength and resources from him. One day we may wake up and find ourselves in a state of confusion and spiritual captivity.

For some Christians, as they come to the realization that they have temporarily, or even for a long period of time, neglected Christ and left the path, they start to backtrack to trace their departure to a particular sin they committed. Sometimes that can be immorality, lying, cheating, stealing, coveting, some unholy alliance, worldliness, pride, an uncontrolled outburst of anger, speaking evil of another brother or sister, or any number of things. But is there a more basic common denominator; some common place of departure, or one common root cause of sin that is the reason for Old Testament and New Testament saint alike to find themselves in spiritual captivity?

God sent his people into Babylon for 70 years. This number was not arbitrary. It was deliberate. It was a specific discipline for a specific offense. The reason for the 70 years is given at the very end of the book of II Chronicles, in II Chronicles 36:20-21: *"until the land had enjoyed its Sabbaths."*

What does the land enjoying its Sabbaths have to do with the captivity? Everything! In spiritual terms, for the Old Testament saint it was their refusal to honor the Sabbatical years and trust in God's provision that resulted in their captivity. For the Christian (or for a group of Christians seeking to follow the Lord together) captivity will result when we fail to rest in Christ and trust in his abundant provision to meet our needs.

WHY KEEPING THE SABBATH WAS SO IMPORTANT

Let me say up front that I am not a Seventh Day Adventist. I do not honor one day above another and I do not deliberately abstain from any kind of work every seventh day. According to Colossians 2:16-17 Paul wrote: "*Therefore no one is to act as your judge in regard to food or drink or in respect to a festival or a new moon or a Sabbath day—things which are a mere shadow of what is to come; but the substance belongs to Christ.*" In the Old Testament, the Sabbath was a picture or a shadow of something to come. That something to come was Christ. He is our real food, our real drink, our real celebration, and our real Sabbath.

To help us understand the reality of what it means to rest in Christ, this Old Testament scenario behind the observance of the Sabbath is so instructive. God gave Israel one day a week for them to remember that they could rest and trust him. Every seventh month he had them observe a feast to remember that they could rest and trust him. Every seventh year he told them that they could take a whole year off to rest and watch him provide for them. Consider these verses:

"You shall sow your land for six years and gather in its yield, but on the seventh year you shall let it rest and lie fallow so that the needy of your people may eat; and whatever they leave the beast

of the field may eat. You are to do the same with your vineyard and your olive grove."

(Exod. 23: 10, 11)

'But if you say, "What are we going to eat on the seventh year if we do not sow or gather in our crops?" then I will so order My blessing for you in the sixth year that it will bring forth crop for three years.'

(Lev. 25: 20-22)

During that seventh year, or the Sabbatical year, the people could fish, hunt, care for their bees and flocks, repair their buildings, make furniture, make clothing, teach one another and their children the ways of God, but God wanted them to let the land rest and he promised to provide for them.

God knows the heart of man. He wanted to demonstrate his love but knew that it would require an act of faith for his people to believe he would provide, even if they didn't plant their crops or tend to their vineyards and trees. So, anticipating that unbelief, he made the promise that in the sixth year, to make up for that seventh year when the ground would lie fallow, that he would provide three times the amount of crops in the sixth year to carry them through.

Think about that! Imagine if you were one of those Israelites. You had a few olive trees on your plot of land, or some grapevines, or a field of wheat. You remember what a normal year's yield is like. But now imagine that your olive tree, your vine, or your wheat field produced three times its normal amount in a single year! Each day before harvest you walk out to see your trees or your vines getting more and more heavy laden with fruit to the point the branches are near to snapping, or your rows of crops getting thicker and taller with sheaves of wheat or barley waving like nothing you've ever seen before. What joy that would produce. What confidence in God's ability and commitment to provide. What praise that would have generated among God's people.

But no. During that whole period of the kings, God's people kept on working. Seventy Sabbatical years went by. They weren't counting, but God was counting. Finally after 490 years had passed—70 Sabbatical years of not honoring the Lord—God sent them into captivity for 70 years, one year for each Sabbatical year they neglected to rest in him and trust in his provision.

God has always wanted man to enter into his rest. Going all the way back to creation, Adam and Eve were created on the sixth day. The day that they woke up was not a day of work, but a day of rest. It was the seventh day, the day God rested. God wanted Adam and Eve to start off by resting with him. In spiritual terms the reason the Israelites were sent into captivity was for their failure to rest in the Lord. The basic lesson that we can learn from this is simple: Rest in the Lord and in his finished work, and trust in his ability to provide.

> *In spiritual terms the reason the Israelites were sent into captivity was for their failure to rest in the Lord. The basic lesson that we can learn from this is simple: Rest in the Lord and in his finished work, and trust in his ability to provide.*

"For thus says the Lord, 'When seventy years have been completed for Babylon, I will visit you and fulfill My good word to you, to bring you back to this place. For I know the plans that I have for you, declares the Lord, plans for welfare and not for calamity, to give you a future and a hope. Then you will call upon Me and come and pray to Me and I will listen to you. You will seek Me

and find Me when you search for Me with all your heart. I will be found by you, declares the Lord, and I will bring you back to the place from where I sent you into exile.'"

(Jer. 29:10-14)

This same principle is clear and consistent throughout the New Testament. In his classic little booklet, *Sit, Walk, Stand,* Watchman Nee pointed out that there are three main sections in the book of Ephesians. The first part deals with a believer's position in Christ. We are seated with him in the heavenly places (Eph. 2:6). Our spiritual life begins with "sitting" and resting in Christ.

The second section of Ephesians deals with our "walk" in the world (4:1), which comes out of our resting in Christ. The third and final section of the book deals with spiritual warfare and our attitude toward the enemy as seen in Ephesians 6:11: *"Put on the full armor of God, so that you will be able to stand firm against the schemes of the devil."* Here Paul used the verb "stand." As Watchman Nee aptly observed, the proper sequence in living out our life with the Lord is to first learn to sit (rest), then walk, and then stand.

TWO GREAT DELIVERANCES IN THE OLD TESTAMENT

Jerusalem means "city of peace." Babylon means "confusion." Ultimately, what happens when the Lord's people stop resting in God and trusting in his provision? They lose their peace and end up in confusion.

When we look at the whole story in the Old Testament, we find that there were two great deliverances for God's people. The first was their deliverance from bondage in Egypt. The second was their deliverance from their captivity in Babylon. In our Christian experience, God wants us to go through both of these deliverances—deliverance from Egypt and deliverance from Babylon. What are the differences?

In Egypt, the people were born there. Through the Passover Lamb, God provided redemption for *everyone* and brought them *all* out of Egypt. Everyone was saved by the blood of the Lamb. All of them had become part of a new nation bound for the Promised Land.

But the deliverance that God provided from Babylon was different. They were in Babylon because they had sinned and they were being disciplined. In Babylon, *all* were invited out, but not all came out. Those who came out had a name. They were known as the remnant.

God wants all of his children to rest in him and let him be the supplier of all their needs. By Christ's work on the cross, we have all had our sins forgiven and have passed from death to life. We all have an inheritance (Christ) that God has prepared for us. But in our walk with Christ, in our life-experience,

> *God wants to deliver us not only from Egypt (representing sin and the flesh), but also from Babylon, which is the place of confusion and man-made religion.*

God wants to deliver us not only from Egypt (representing sin and the flesh), but also from Babylon, which is the place of confusion and man-made religion. He wants to return us all to Jerusalem, where spiritually we can abide with him in a place of peace and rest. There in Jerusalem he wants to restore the temple, rebuild a wall of security and protection for his people, and establish a government and a kingdom. As we will see in the book of Ezra it is God's heart desire for all of his people to return to the land of their inheritance and be part of the rebuilding process. The book of Ezra begins with a proclamation from King Cyrus saying, *"Whoever there is among you of all His people, may his God be with him! Let him go up to Jerusalem which is in Judah and rebuild the house of the Lord, the God of Israel; He is the God who is in Jerusalem" (Ezra 1:3).* Cyrus issued the call to *all*, but not all returned.

Who was this Cyrus? In the next chapter we'll look more closely at the life of this man and the extraordinary circumstances under which God raised him up. This should teach us something about God's faithfulness and about his steadfast desire that his people be fully restored.

Chapter Three

A Classic Example of God's Sovereignty
King Cyrus

Now in the first year of Cyrus king of Persia—in order to fulfill the word of the Lord by the mouth of Jeremiah—the Lord stirred up the spirit of Cyrus king of Persia, so that he sent out a proclamation throughout his kingdom, and also put it in writing, saying, "Thus says Cyrus King of Persia, 'The Lord, the God of heaven, has given me all the kingdoms of the earth, and He has appointed me to build Him a house in Jerusalem, which is in Judah. Whoever there is among you of all His people, may the Lord his God be with him, and let him go up!'"

(II Chron. 36:22, 23)

Cyrus was the founder of the Persian Empire. Jeremiah had prophesied that the Jews would be taken into captivity for 70 years, and then return to the land of Canaan. He also prophesied that at the end of those 70 years God would judge the Babylonians. Cyrus was the instrument God used to fulfill both of these prophesies.

Cyrus, a Persian (modern-day Iran), defeated the Medians, the kingdom of Lydia, and the Assyrians, and in 538 B.C. conquered the Babylonians. He was welcomed as a liberator with cheers from its citizenry. In the same year he issued this great proclamation we read about in II Chronicles and also in the first chapter of Ezra, granting those in captivity in Babylon the opportunity to return to their homeland and rebuild the house of God in Jerusalem.

This seems quite unusual that a victorious king who was not a Jew, who had just defeated the Babylonians, consolidated his kingdom, and become the most powerful ruler on earth would place such a high priority in the first year of his reign on allowing the Jews go back to Jerusalem to rebuild their temple. What was behind this decision? What do we know about Cyrus? Was he a believer? This is what we do know.

Cyrus is first mentioned in the Bible well before the year 538, the year he issued his proclamation. We first read about Cyrus in chapter 44 of the book of Isaiah where Isaiah records the Lord speaking to his people,

> *Thus says the Lord, your Redeemer, the one who formed you from the womb..."It is I who says of Cyrus, 'He is My shepherd! And he will perform all My desire.' And he declares of Jerusalem, 'She will be built,' And of the temple, 'Your foundation will be laid.'"*
>
> (Isa. 44:24, 28)

Here the Lord calls Cyrus "*My shepherd.*" Cyrus was a chosen instrument of God. Isaiah chapter 45 goes on to say:

> *Thus says the Lord to Cyrus His anointed. Whom I have taken by the right hand, to subdue nations before him and to loose the loins of kings; to open doors before him so that gates will not be*

shut: "I will go before you and make the rough places smooth; I will shatter the doors of bronze and cut through their iron bars. I will give you the treasures of darkness and hidden wealth of secret places, so that you may know that it is I, the Lord, the God of Israel, who calls you by your name. For the sake of Jacob My servant, and Israel My chosen, I have also called you by your name; I have given you a title of honor though you have not known Me. I am the Lord, and there is no other; besides Me there is no God. I will gird you, though you have not known Me; that men may know from the rising to the setting of the sun that there is no one besides Me. I am the Lord, and there is no other, the one forming light and creating darkness, causing well-being and creating calamity; I am the Lord who does all these."

(Isa. 45:1-7)

In this passage God calls Cyrus *"His anointed."* He promises to subdue nations before him, to go before him, to make his path smooth, to give him success, victory, wealth, and honor. The remarkable thing is that he promised all these things to a man who did not know him—to a Gentile, Persian king! Why would God do this? In Isaiah's own words, *"...that men may know from the rising to the setting of the sun that there is no one besides Me. I am the Lord, and there is no other..."*

What makes this passage even more than remarkable and launches it into the realm of the incredible is that these prophesies were recorded 175 years before Cyrus was even born! Long before Cyrus breathed his first breath of air, God introduced him to the world. Almost 200 years before this man

Long before Cyrus breathed his first breath of air, God introduced him to the world. Almost 200 years before this man became king, the prophet Isaiah called him by name.

became king, the prophet Isaiah called him by name. That is amazing!

Shouldn't that comfort us and remind us that God is really in control? That God really knows the future? That God knows *our* futures?

THE ROLE OF DANIEL IN CYRUS' LIFE

Fast forward from the time of Isaiah's prophesies to the time of Nebuchadnezzar. Nebuchadnezzar had commissioned several raids against Jerusalem, but the culmination victory occurred in 586 B.C. when he destroyed Jerusalem and took thousands of POWs back to Babylon. One of those POWs was a young man named Daniel.

Daniel grew up in a royal family in Jerusalem. Very early in the 70-year captivity, and well before Cyrus' decree, Daniel was singled out along with some others to serve Nebuchadnezzar because he was good looking, intelligent, full of knowledge, and a young man endowed with natural leadership abilities. As Daniel grew in stature in the king's court, the Lord also added to his abilities the supernatural gift of interpreting dreams. In time, Nebuchadnezzar made Daniel ruler of the whole province of Babylon. Later, during Darius' reign, Daniel was given first place as one of the three rulers of the empire. In addition to these responsibilities, he was also made the custodian over all the Jewish writings that were taken from the temple in Jerusalem.

When Nebuchadnezzar died, Belshazzar, his son, replaced him as ruler. One night Belshazzar called for a feast, and at that dinner party the fingers of a man's hand appeared and began writing on the wall of the palace. The king was frightened and called for the fortune tellers to interpret the writing. He announced that anyone who could interpret this event would be given honor and the authority to rule one-third of the kingdom, but none of his wise men could interpret the writing. Finally Daniel was summoned to interpret the handwriting.

Daniel told Belshazzar that because he had not humbled himself and had exalted himself against the God of heaven, God had put an end to his kingdom and given it over to the Medes and Persians. In that same night Belshazzar was slain and Darius the Mede received the kingdom (in the interim before Cyrus).

Darius honored Daniel, but some of his officials plotted against Daniel and accused him before Darius of praying to his God, which according to a document Darius was persuaded to sign, was against the law and any violator would be cast into the lions den.

But God miraculously delivered Daniel from being killed and eaten in the lion's den, and once again Darius highly exalted him:

> *Then Darius the king wrote to all the peoples, nations and men of every language who were living in all the land: "May your peace abound! I make a decree that in all the dominion of my kingdom men are to fear and tremble before the God of Daniel: For He is the living God and enduring forever, and his kingdom is one which will not be destroyed, and his dominion will be forever. He delivers and rescues and performs signs and wonders in heaven and on earth, Who has also delivered Daniel from the power of the lions."*
>
> (Dan. 6:25-28)

So Daniel enjoyed great success and honor and was well known and respected in the kings' courts leading up to the overthrow of the Babylonian Empire by King Cyrus of Persia.

History does not record for us how Daniel met Cyrus. But from the onset of Cyrus' rule, Daniel had access to the king.

Imagine for a moment what must have gone through Daniel's mind as he saw King Cyrus, a heathen king, rise to power. Daniel was the custodian of the Hebrew writings. He was well acquainted with Jeremiah's prophesy concerning the 70-year captivity and knew that the time for restoration was at hand. But he was equally familiar with the writings of the prophet Isaiah written 200 years earlier naming Cyrus by name and calling him God's Servant; God's Anointed.

So Daniel opened the Scriptures for King Cyrus. The realization that the God of the universe knew him by name, had raised him up, brought him to power, given him great wealth, and so intertwined his life with the fate of the Jewish people must have blown Cyrus away! His response is recorded in both II Chronicles 36:22, 23 and in Ezra 1: 1-4:

> *Now in the first year of Cyrus king of Persia, in order to fulfill the word of the Lord by the mouth of Jeremiah, the Lord stirred up the spirit of Cyrus king of Persia, so that he sent a proclamation throughout all his kingdom, and also put it in writing, saying; "Thus says Cyrus king of Persia, 'The Lord, the God of heaven, has given me all the kingdoms of the earth and he has appointed me to build him a house in Jerusalem, which is in Judah. Whoever there is among you of all his people, may his God be with him! Let him go up to Jerusalem which is in Judah and rebuild the house of the Lord, the God of Israel; He is the God who is in Jerusalem. Every survivor, at whatever place he may live, let the men of that place support him with silver and gold, with goods and cattle, together with a freewill offering for the house of God which is in Jerusalem.'"*
>
> (Ezra 1:1-4)

Cyrus made a proclamation and the message was sent throughout his kingdom. He even put it in writing so that everyone would not only hear about it, but be able to read it. In Ezra 1:7-11 it even says that he brought out the articles of the house of the Lord that Nebuchadnezzar had carried away from Jerusalem, and sent them back with remnant. He authorized the financial support for this undertaking so all the bills would be paid. This is an incredible passage that reveals God's faithfulness, foresight, sovereignty, predetermined plan, and that he would provide for it all.

What must it have been like for the people living at the time of this proclamation? Picture yourself as a Jewish man living in the days of King Cyrus. You live in the small, Egyptian fishing village of Rhakotis, along the shores of the Mediterranean Sea (later to be the site of the modern city of Alexandria). A generation ago your family fled from Israel and settled here. Word comes to you and the others in your village that King Cyrus has issued this astonishing proclamation.

You rush home and inform your wife Hadassah, your three small children, and your relatives of the opportunity for all of you to return to your homeland. You are thrilled beyond belief.

Hadassah reluctantly buys into the idea but the first thing on her mind is, "How are we going to afford this?"

"Don't worry," you say. "King Cyrus also proclaimed that the men of this village must support us with silver and gold, cattle and food, and everything we will need for our journey back. They've also been commanded to make a freewill offering to help rebuild the house of God in Jerusalem!"

You and Hadassah pray about it. You have peace and joy in your hearts to return. But some of your other relatives in that village have concerns and are not convinced. Still, you know that you and your family must go.

All the people were invited to go back. But how many actually responded?

In Ezra 1:5 we read: "*The heads of fathers' households of Judah and Benjamin and the priests and the Levites arose, even everyone whose spirit God had stirred to go up and rebuild the house of the Lord which is in Jerusalem.*"

All were invited to go back, all heard and could read the proclamation, but not all went back. Everything was to be provided, but only a remnant of about 50,000 people actually returned.

To summarize, this is the background leading up to the book of Ezra:

> *All were invited to go back, all heard and could read the proclamation, but not all went back. Everything was to be provided, but only a remnant of about 50,000 people actually returned.*

- God is sovereign.
- God is in control.
- God has compassion on his people.
- It was God's faithfulness, not the faithfulness of the people that initiated the return and the rebuilding of the temple.
- God's desire for his people was that they return and rebuild the temple, the wall, and the city.
- A proclamation was made for everyone to hear and to read.
- It was an unconditional invitation for everyone who had refused rest but who now wanted to leave confusion to go back to the city of peace.

- Only a portion returned. Only a remnant responded and went back to Jerusalem to fulfill the heartbeat, the plan, and the purpose of God, which was to have a people on this earth, a temple, a testimony, and a place where he could dwell and establish his kingdom.

PUTTING THE BOOK OF EZRA IN CONTEXT

Before actually getting into the book of Ezra, there is something else we need to see concerning the period it covers in order to really understand and appreciate what was going on at the time. The book of Ezra covers approximately the last 100 years of the history of Israel recorded in the Old Testament. Ezra himself does not appear in the book for approximately 80 years—toward the very end.

Chronologically, the writings covering this period of the rebuilding of the temple, the rebuilding of the wall, and the restoration of the city are found in the books of Ezra and Nehemiah. Chapters one through six of Ezra deal with the return from captivity and the rebuilding of the temple. Then there is a gap of about 57-58 years. Following that gap we come to Ezra chapters seven through ten and then the story continues in the book of Nehemiah, where we see the completion of the wall and the reinhabiting of the city.

What happened during that 57 year gap in the history? For one thing, the book of Esther was written during that time. The setting for the book of Esther was Babylon, specifically the city of Susa, and the cast were all those who had not left Babylon but had remained in their captivity and not returned to Jerusalem.

So historically and chronologically, we have:

- The book of Ezra (chapters one through six)
- The book of Esther (between chapters six and seven of Ezra)
- The book of Ezra (chapters seven through ten)
- The book of Nehemiah

The three other books that are closely related to the book of Ezra and help to put it in context are the books of Haggai, Zechariah, and Malachi. These prophets all lived during this same time period and prophesied to the remnant. Here are some dates that will help us navigate through that first segment of the book of Ezra from the time when the work on the temple began to when it was completed.

538: The decree by Cyrus.

536: The remnant came back and began work on the temple.

534: They had erected the altar and the foundation of the temple had been laid, but they received opposition from their local neighbors, the Samaritans, and the work stopped. For about 15 years the work of completing the temple was disregarded.

521: Haggai and Zechariah began to prophesy.

520: The work resumed.

516: The temple was completed.

It took a total of about 20 years from the time the remnant began work on the temple to the time they completed it. The altar was erected and the foundation was completed in the first two years, but following that the work ceased for 15 years. What made the people stop building after getting off to such a good start? And why, at the end of those 15 years, did they resume again? We'll explore the answers to those questions in subsequent chapters but the two most significant events that got them back on track again were the arrival of two prophets. God raised up Haggai and Zechariah to prophesy to the remnant. After hearing from the prophets, the people were stirred

What made the people stop building after getting off to such a good start? And why, at the end of those 15 years, did they resume again?

up. They were revived. They got their focus back and returned to the work, and in only four years the temple was completed.

By looking at all of these books as a whole—Ezra, Nehemiah, Haggai, Zechariah, and Malachi—and how they relate to one another, by God's grace, we should be able to gain some insight concerning what the Lord wants to show us about the restoration and rebuilding of the house of God in our day.

Chapter Four

COMFORTABLE IN CAPTIVITY
LIFE IN BABYLON

Therefore the redeemed of the Lord shall return and come with singing unto Zion. An everlasting joy shall be upon their heads.

(Isa. 51:11)

How lovely on the mountains are the feet of him who brings good news. Who announces peace and brings good news of happiness, who announces salvation and says to Zion, "Your God reigns!" Listen! Your watchmen lift up their voices, they shout joyfully together; for they will see with their own eyes when the Lord restores Zion. Break forth, shout joyfully together, you waste places of Jerusalem; for the Lord has comforted his people, he has redeemed Jerusalem. The Lord has bared his holy arm in the sight of all the nations that all the ends of the earth may see the salvation of our God.

(Isa. 52:7)

By the rivers of Babylon, there we sat down and wept, when we remembered Zion. Upon the willows in the midst of it we hung our harps. For there our captors demanded of us songs, and our tormentors mirth, saying, "Sing us one of the songs of Zion." How can we sing the Lord's song a foreign land? If I forget you, O Jerusalem, May my right hand forget her skill. May my tongue cling to the roof of my mouth if I do not remember you, if I do not exalt Jerusalem above my chief joy.

(Ps. 137:1-6)

There was no joy for those taken away into captivity in Babylon. Over the 70-year period prior to the remnant's return, many of the Jews may have grown to be secure, comfortable, busy, occupied, even successful and prosperous, but there was no joy and God's house still lay in ruin.

Don't we see this in the church today? Christians who have grown secure, comfortable, successful in their businesses or jobs, focused on building a nest egg for their retirement, seemingly happy and content, but with no joy, no longing to see God's house restored, and no lament that his house lies in ruins.

THE CITY OF BABEL

The roots of the Babylonian Empire can ultimately be traced to the city of Babel, first mentioned in Genesis chapter 11. Babel became the capital of the country referred to as Shinar, and later the land of the Chaldeans.

Babel's notoriety was the fact that it was the city of false religion, where man attempted to reach God through his own efforts. There fallen man built a city with a tower made of brick and mortar that extended into the heavens. Symbolically, brick is something man-made. By contrast, when God's temple was built, it was made with stone, not something man-made but something God himself created.

In man's building the bricks were held together by mortar. What does mortar represent? Mortar represents the rules, regulations, rituals, and legalism that are required to hold a group of people together. This man-made building or tower in Babylon projected an appearance of godliness and unity, but this was not God's way of building. It was a building based on human effort. It was a counterfeit and ultimately had to be brought down. It ended in confusion and division.

Spiritually, God's purpose is to build people together by his Spirit, with his own life, not by rules, regulations, and human ingenuity. He is our unity. His goal is ultimately to build himself into his people and to manifest the love of God among them in such a way that the high-priestly prayer of the Lord Jesus recorded in John chapter 17 will be realized:

> *"I do not ask on behalf of these alone (the disciples), but for those also who believe in Me through their word; that they may all be one; even as You, Father, are in Me and I in You, that they also may be in Us, that the world may believe that You sent Me."*
> (John 17:20-21)

Paul contrasts the building work of God with the building work of man in the following passage from I Corinthians:

> *For we are God's fellow workers; you are God's field, you are God's building. According to the grace of God which was given to me, as a wise master builder I have laid the foundation, and another builds on it. But let each one take heed how he builds on it. For no other foundation can anyone lay than that which is laid, which is Jesus Christ. Now if anyone builds on this foundation with gold, silver, precious stones, wood, hay, straw, each one's*

work will become clear; for the Day will declare it, because it will be revealed by fire; and the fire will test each one's work, of what sort it is. If anyone's work which he has built on it endures, he will receive a reward. If anyone's work is burned, he will suffer loss; but he himself will be saved, yet so as through fire.

(I Corinthians 3:9-15)

Where God is at work and building people together there is always a sense of freedom, life, and joy. Man's work for God produces a sense of obligation and duty, resulting in lack of joy and confusion. Because it was God's work that brought the remnant back to Jerusalem to rebuild the temple, the people returned with great joy.

> *Where God is at work and building people together there is always a sense of freedom, life, and joy.*

Can we see any application of this for us as Christians today? What are we to do when we find that we have slipped into a condition where we've lost our peace and joy? Why can Christianity sometimes seem like it's only a set of rules to obey, or observing the same rituals over and over again? What could have happened to cause hearts, once on fire for the Lord, to grow cold and make serving God seem a boring drudgery?

We can find ourselves in this state for a variety of reasons. It can happen as a result of outright sin, or we can just gradually slip away from God. Often it develops as a result of our feeling that we need to do something for God; that if we clean ourselves up by doing good works, or if we fast more, deny ourselves certain foods, don't go to the movies or play video games, that this will make us better Christians. It may be brought on by the circumstances we find ourselves in, by the trials we face, by the bad news we received, by the difficult relationships we are in, or by some disappointment or failure. All of these things may contribute, but ultimately we lose our peace and joy and find ourselves back in the city of confusion for the same reason the Jews woke up one day and found themselves in Babylon. They had neglected to observe the Sabbath rest. For us, we lose our peace and joy when we stop resting and abiding in Christ and cease trusting in his finished work and provision.

When we find ourselves in such a condition, we need to be revived. We need to be brought back. We need to have our peace and our joy restored.

THREE REVIVALS EXPERIENCED BY THE REMNANT

During this last 100 years of recorded Old Testament history when the temple was rebuilt, the walls around Jerusalem were rebuilt, and the city was re-populated and restored, there were three revivals that took place among God's people. The word revival means "to live again."

We can find three corresponding revivals that we need to experience as Christians. When we first become Christians and are "born again" we are given life from above and we begin really living for the first time. But in the Christian experience, there are times when the fire seems to go out and we need to be revived.

While on a trip to Turkey in 2005 I was waiting in the airport in Istanbul for a flight and ended up sitting next to a Mormon man. We passed the time in conversation and I remember talking with him about the movie, *The Passion of Christ*. He asked me if I liked it. I told him that I did and that it had made a profound impression on me. Then he said, "Yea, I wanted to go, but I decided a long time ago that I would never go to a movie that had an 'R' rating."

I am not criticizing this man's heart. His heart was to please God. But the way in which he was trying to do it was by keeping a bunch of self-imposed rules. He was in bondage. He was not free.

What happens when we as Christians lose our peace, lose our relationship with God, lose our joy, and find ourselves in the land of confusion and man-made religion? Why is it that we can be doing all the right religious things that we're supposed to do as Christians, but without joy? What do we need? We need revival. We need to "live again." We need the same revival that the remnant returning from Babylon experienced. We need to get out of Babylon and return to Jerusalem. We need to leave the place of man-made religion and return to the city of peace with other believers of like mind, set up the altar, and begin rebuilding the temple of God once again on its original foundation. When the people responded to God's call, they came back with great joy, as the prophet Isaiah predicted.

The second revival came about 15 years later. After the remnant had returned and started building, they ran into some problems from their local neighbors and the building came to a halt. But at the end of those 15 years the people started building again and in four years the temple was complete. The people were revived. What precipitated this second revival? What caused them to go back to work again? What caused them to continue to grow and go on with the Lord? It was the arrival of the two prophets, Haggai and Zechariah. In order to understand this revival and what was really happening during this period, we'll need to look at the messages of these two prophets, which we will do in a later chapter. But the messages they delivered gave the people renewed vision and strength to return to the task.

Finally, the third revival came about 80 years after they had first returned, and after they had finished the wall under the leadership of Nehemiah. This revival is seen in Ezra chapter seven through Nehemiah chapter ten. This brought a third wave of joy and rejoicing.

Maybe as a Christian you've already experienced revival number one in your life, having lost your freedom in Christ for a while, but then having been delivered from the land of confusion back into the land of peace. And maybe you've already experienced revival number two, having received revelation from God's prophets that has stirred you, reinforced your commitment to Christ, and brought you to new levels of Christian maturity. But still there is more for you to experience in your journey with Christ. There is revival number three. This came for the people when they finally came to the stage where they were hearing the Word of God for themselves.

Have you found this to be true in your own life? I recall as a young believer how hungry I was for the Word of God. I had such an appetite to hear men of God teach the Scriptures. I couldn't get enough of it. This is where we all begin.

But the time comes in our lives when God wants to move us beyond being dependent on hearing the Word of God as it comes to us from others. He desires to bring us to the point where we can hear from him ourselves. He wants to speak to us and for us to be able to hear his voice. He wants us to be able to receive revelation from his Spirit and from the Scriptures for ourselves.

As Job testified after all of his trials, *"I have heard of You by the hearing of the ear; But now my eye sees You (Job 42:5).* This is the third revival that the remnant experienced, and something that God desires to bring about in the lives of all of his children.

THE SYNAGOGUE SYSTEM

II Chronicles 36:17 says that when Jerusalem was taken by the Babylonians they slew the young men, had no compassion on the young men, the virgins, the old men, or the infirm. Most everyone in Jerusalem lost some family member or relative. Verse 20 in the same chapter says that those who escaped the sword were taken away and became servants.

If you read through the book of Lamentations, you'll find Jeremiah's description of the captivity. The Jews were completely stripped of their dignity. They were marched 700 miles in the nude to Babylon. The Babylonians gave them new names and at first, many of their children starved to death. Their women were raped. In chapter one of Lamentations, Jeremiah described how the princess (the daughter of Zion) had become a forced laborer and that Judah had gone into exile under affliction and harsh servitude. The people were portrayed as having tears running down their cheeks, finding no rest, unable to celebrate their feasts, and full of groaning. Lamentations 5:10-21 describes the situation this way:

Our skin has become as hot as an oven because of the burning heat of famine. They ravished the women in Zion, the virgins in the cities of Judah. Princes were hung by their hands; elders were not respected. Young men worked at the grinding mill, and youths stumbled under loads of wood. Elders are gone from the gate; young men from their music. The joy of our hearts has ceased; our dancing has been turned into mourning. The crown has fallen from our head; woe to us, for we have sinned! Because of this our heart is faint, because of these things our eyes are dim; because of Mount Zion which lies desolate, foxes prowl in it. You, O Lord, rule forever: Your throne is from generation to generation. Why do You forget us forever? Why do You forsake us so long? Restore us to You, O Lord, that we may be restored; renew our days as of old.

To say that things started out pretty bleak is an understatement. Gradually, however, these slaves were given considerable freedom in Babylon. They built houses, some started businesses, and many prospered. There was relative religious freedom. And since they had no temple at which to worship, it was there in Babylon that the Jews invented their own religious system that exists down to this day: the synagogue system. These are some of the characteristics that governed synagogue worship:

- To qualify to start a synagogue only required 10 men.
- Synagogues stood, if possible, on the highest ground in or near the city to which it belonged. When people entered the structure, they faced and prayed toward Jerusalem. (Moslems today, facing Mecca when they bow down to pray, certainly can't be credited for coming up with anything original.)
- At the Jerusalem end of the building, close to where the Book of the Law was located, were the places of honor and the chief seats where the Pharisees and scribes delighted to sit and be recognized. We read about this practice even in the New Testament in Matthew 23:6. It was also the place where wealthy and honored guests were invited to sit (James 2:2, 3).
- Congregations were divided with men seated on one side and women on the other. Normally a five to six foot partition was erected between them. From what I have read (although I am no expert) one style of synagogue placed the women in low side-galleries, screened off by lattice

work, exactly what we see in the way Muslims worship in mosques today.

- A synagogue could be started anywhere. It was very convenient because people didn't have to travel far to get to meetings to worship, as opposed to Jerusalem, where they may have needed to travel a great distance to get to the temple.

- If a person didn't like certain people, he could get nine other men to follow him and they could start another synagogue.

- Even in the apostles' times there were synagogues of the guilds in Jerusalem—mason's synagogues, mechanics synagogues, even, I suppose, actors synagogues.

- At the synagogues they read from the Torah, the Prophets, sang Psalms, and prayed. First in the sequence of their order of worship, the whole Law was read consecutively so as to be completed over a three-year cycle. Then the Prophets were read, followed by a sermon (Acts 13:15). There was a great deal of liberty at these synagogue meetings. In the time of the apostles, a new person could come into a synagogue and say what he wanted to say (Paul, as an example—Acts 13:14, 15).

This all sounds very practical and convenient. The only trouble was that they couldn't offer sacrifice. The Law said that without the shedding of blood there is no remission for sin. The shedding of blood was restricted to the altar at the temple, and the location for the temple was back in Jerusalem. In the synagogue they could feel religious and perform religious duties but they could not restore their relationship with God through sacrifice. The people in Babylon had become self-centered and comfortable, but the only place that God had designated for sacrifice and where he would have his name was in Jerusalem, the city of peace.

It's interesting to observe that even people who have been in prison for a long time begin feeling comfortable in that environment, even to the point that they can become afraid when faced with the possibility of being released. Similarly in Babylon, when the invitation was issued by Cyrus to go back to Jerusalem to rebuild the temple and get back to God's heart and God's design, the majority chose to remain in their captivity and passed up the invitation.

> *It's interesting to observe that even people who have been in prison for a long time begin feeling comfortable in that environment, even to the point that they can become afraid when faced with the possibility of being released.*

GOD'S HEART WAS TO SEE THEM COME BACK

"I will rejoice over them to do them good and will faithfully plant them in this land with all My heart and with all My soul. For thus says the Lord, 'Just as I brought all this great disaster on this people, so I am going to bring on them all the good that I am promising them.'"

(Jer. 32:41, 42)

God's whole heart and soul was for them to return to the land of their inheritance. He promised to bring good upon them. All received the invitation. The full price was paid. But only about 50,000 returned.

History tells us that God has always worked through a remnant. A prime example of that can be seen when God delivered the people from the land of Egypt. His original intent for them was to make them a nation of priests (Exod. 19), but because the majority of the people sinned and rebelled, only the tribe of Levi was chosen to maintain the priesthood on behalf of the whole nation.

ZERUBBABEL, THE REMNANT LEADER

Some explanation is needed as to who led this group of people back from Babylon to Jerusalem. In Ezra 1:7 we come across the name "Sheshbazzar." Later, in Ezra 15:14-16, we see that he is credited with laying the foundation of the temple.

Who was this Sheshbazzar? According to Zechariah 4:9, Zerubbabel was the one who laid the foundation. This means that Sheshbazzar and Zerubbabel were the same person. Just like Daniel who was given a Babylonian name but also kept his Jewish name, the same was true with Zerubbabel. So when you see the names Sheshbazzar and Zerubbabel in these remnant books, they are interchangeable and always refer to the same person.

The name "Zerubbabel" means "born in Babylon, but does not belong" or it could also be translated, "stranger in Babylon." As Zerubbabel grew up as a young lad in captivity with his family, every morning that his parents called him to the breakfast table by his Hebrew name, they would be reminding him, "Son, you don't belong here."

Zerubbabel hadn't seen the original temple. He was the grandson of Jehoiachin, one of the kings of Judah who had been taken to captivity. At the end of the book of II Kings it says that the king of Babylon (Nebuchadnezzar) retrieved Jehoiachin from prison and made him a personal friend. So Jehoiachin must have lived in or near to the Royal Palace. Zerubbabel, being his grandson, must have grown up there as well. And if he grew up around the royal palace, he must have also known Daniel. Daniel was an old man and probably talked a lot about the temple in Jerusalem. Combining what Zerubbabel was taught from his grandfather and from Daniel, he must have grown up with an appetite to learn everything he could about the temple and with a burden in his heart that if the time ever came to go back, he would be one of the first to go.

As we consider Zerubbabel's leadership in bringing the remnant back to Jerusalem, we might ask ourselves, what kind of leaders will it take to lead God's people out of the fallen situation Christianity is in today? Most likely, they will be leaders with hearts like Zerubbabel's. They will be people with a hunger and passion to study the first-century church and understand the Scriptures in a way that those early believers, who were recipients of those letters, understood them. They will be people who don't fit in the present religious system—probably individuals who could be misinterpreted as being mavericks or rebels, but definitely those who know that though they may have been raised in Babylon, they don't belong there. The kinds of leaders that it will take to lead God's people out of today's Babylon and back to Jerusalem will not be those who just have some good ideas or theories, but they must be people of vision.

> *The kinds of leaders that it will take to lead God's people out of to-day's Babylon and back to Jerusalem will not be those who just have some good ideas or theories, but they must be people of vision.*

WHO RETURNED TO REBUILD

The remnant that returned to rebuild returned with great joy and anticipation. They made the 700-mile journey by foot.

It took them six months to a year to get back to Jerusalem, and
when they got there, the place was in complete ruin. For those of
us in America, it would have been like coming back to Ground
Zero in New York and finding the rubble of the Twin Towers
that had been destroyed on 9/11. There in Jerusalem, the walls
had been torn down and the gates burned out. There was rubble
everywhere. Weeds had engulfed the former building site.

Ezra chapter two records who came back. That list includes
priests, Levites, singers, servants, and gatekeepers. These were
the ones who said "yes" to God's invitation. The same list is
repeated in Nehemiah. It requires all kinds of people with different gifting to rebuild the house of God. Are you a priest?
Are you one who earnestly seeks God? You may come. Are you
a Levite? Are you one of those assigned to assist and help the
priests by performing practical duties? You may come. Are you
a singer? The house of God needs singers. Are you a servant?
The house of God needs servants—many servants. Are you a
gatekeeper—one who keeps the bad guys out? God needs your
type. God needs all kinds of people who are willing to leave everything—their security, comfort, man-made religious practices,
synagogues—and come back with other people of like mind
and a common purpose to rebuild his house.

WHO ELSE RETURNED? THE FAILURES RETURNED

In Ezra 2:61-63 we read that some of the priests who came
back were excluded from the priesthood because they could not
produce the records of their genealogy. The Jews kept meticu-
lous records of their genealogies in order to be able to trace the
genealogy of the Messiah. The ones who had lost their genealogies were considered unclean and excluded from the priesthood. The sons of Barzillai (verse 61) were among those. They

were descendants of a priest who let his son marry the heathen daughter of Barzillai (a Gileadite) and allowed that family to take on the heathen name.

The big problem for these sons of Barzillai was that they were descendents of Levi. Going all the way back to the times of Moses, the Levites were the priestly tribe. All of the other tribes of Israel were given a portion of the land of Canaan as their inheritance, but the Levites were given no land as their inheritance. Their inheritance was God himself (Numbers 18:20; Deut. 10:9).

The sons of Barzillai had dropped the name that would have given them their legal status as Levites. The only remedy and hope for their situation and their restoration to their former standing was said to be in the shedding of divine light from the stones on the breastplate of the priest, the Urim and the Thummim.

We learn from this that their restoration to their former standing was totally up to God to decide. Were they a part of the remnant? Yes. Were they numbered among those who responded to God's call and returned. Yes. Could they be fully restored to their former capacity as Levites and priests? That would be dependent on God's supernatural illumination. It was up to God to prove who they were and it was up to God whether or not they would be restored to their former priestly ministry or occupy some other capacity of service among those who returned.

How can we apply this to the situation today? Some people may feel that they have failed so miserably in the past that there is no hope for them. They gave up on God at some point in their lives, turned their back on him, and threw away their inheritance. But God wants to restore all his children. Look at the story of the Prodigal Son. He had squandered his inheritance, but God welcomed him back.

If you are one of those who thinks that you messed up so badly in the past that you are not worthy to come back to be a part of the rebuilding of the house of God, then consider this record. God would have you back. Your name is on the guest list too. Will God immediately and completely restore you to the place of responsibility and ministry that you had before? That is up to God. But are you welcomed back? Yes, you are welcome to be a part of his rebuilding and restoration work.

> *If you are one of those who thinks that you messed up so badly in the past that you are not worthy to come back to be a part of the rebuilding of the house of God, then consider this record. God would have you back. Your name is on the guest list too.*

Chapter Five

WHERE DO WE START?
REBUILDING THE TEMPLE: THE ALTAR AND THE FOUNDATION

Some of the heads of the fathers' households, when they arrived at the house of the Lord which is in Jerusalem, offered willingly for the house of God to restore it on its (original) foundation.

(Ezra 2:68)

Now when the seventh month came, and the sons of Israel were in the cities, the people gathered together as one man to Jerusalem.

(Ezra 3:1)

Therefore I urge you, brethren, by the mercies of God, to present your bodies a living and holy sacrifice, acceptable to God, which is your spiritual service of worship.

(Rom. 12:1)

Then Jeshua the son of Jozadak and his brothers and the priests, and Zerubbabel the son of Shealtiel and his brothers arose and built the altar of the God of Israel to offer burnt offerings on it,

as it is written in the law of Moses, the man of God. So they set
up the altar on its foundations, for they were terrified because of
the peoples of the lands; and they offered burnt offerings on it to
the Lord, burnt offerings morning and evening.

(Ezra 3:2, 3)

They celebrated the Feast of Booths.

(Ezra 3:4)

Now when the builders had laid the foundation of the temple of
the Lord, the priests stood in their apparel with trumpets, and
the Levites, the sons of Asaph, with cymbals, to praise the Lord
according to the directions of King David of Israel. They sang,
praising and giving thanks to the Lord, saying, "For He is good,
for His lovingkindness is upon Israel forever." And all the people
shouted with a great shout when they praised the Lord because
the foundation of the house of the Lord was laid. Yet many of
the priests and Levites and the heads of fathers' households, the
old men who had seen the first temple, wept with a loud voice
when the foundation of this house was laid before their eyes,
while many shouted aloud for joy, so that the people could not
distinguish the sound of the shout of joy from the sound of the
weeping of the people, for the people shouted with a loud shout,
and the sound was heard far away.

(Ezra 3:10-13)

In Ezra 2:68 it says that the remnant returned to restore the
house of God on its original foundation. What does that mean
to us today?

Over the past 2,000 years much has been added to the
practice of the Christian church that was not a part of the first-
century believers' experience. I've often wondered how the
apostle Paul would react if he could have been transported in
a time machine and stepped out onto an intersection on main

street USA, on a Sunday morning in the year 2007, where on each street corner there was a building with some name written on it ending in "church." I could imagine him accompanying an unsuspecting church-goer into one of the buildings, sitting down on a pew alongside of him, and after a few minutes of bewilderment, leaning over and asking his new-found friend, "What's going on here? What are all these people doing?"

People living in the 21st century who become Christians cannot escape having preconceptions of what Christianity is, or what the church is about. (Exceptions would be those people primarily in what are considered to be third-world countries—or in mission terminology, the 10/40 window. There, pioneer church planting is still alive and well. Heralds of the gospel often arrive in cities, towns, and villages where the name of Jesus Christ and the word "church" have never been in circulation. In places like this there are no preconceptions of what the practice of the church is supposed to look like.)

Folks in America have grown up around church buildings. Most people have probably visited some, or at least seen a portion of a church service on the television. They're accustomed to buildings with crosses on them and church leaders that dress well and assume respectable titles. They're familiar with the large churches, especially the Catholic and Anglican churches, with all of their pomp, ceremony, and the costumes worn by their high officials. This form of Christianity has been part of the landscape and in the mindset of believers since the Pilgrims first stepped foot off the boat, but it has no origin in the first-century church.

Even a casual reading of the New Testament reveals a

Even a casual reading of the New Testament reveals a practice of Christianity that has little in common with the way in which it is practiced today.

practice of Christianity that has little in common with the way in which it is practiced today. For centuries God has been raising up people and groups who have challenged the conventional practices of the day, who have left institutional structures in quest of a purer, undefiled, Spirit-led, New Testament-based practice of their faith.

As we study the books of Ezra and Nehemiah, we can take comfort in the fact that God has had a remnant throughout the ages that found themselves living in a foreign land with regard to the institutionalized religion of their days. Thankfully, we have this example in the Old Testament Scriptures showing us how God touched people's lives by his Spirit and drew them to embark on a the journey that led them back to be about the business of restoring his house.

The first thing that should be clear as we approach the book of Ezra is that though God issued a call to all of his people living in Babylon to return to Jerusalem and rebuild his house, not many responded. Unfortunately, we find the same thing true today. Many Christians are content to remain where they are, even if they're aware that their church situation is far from where it ought to be and has lost its vitality and life.

THE ORIGINAL FOUNDATION: CHRIST

In the book of Ezra we read that the remnant returned to the place of God's choice to rebuild the temple *on its original foundation.* For New Testament believers Paul drew on that analogy in I Corinthians to explain the foundation upon which all true Christian ministry is based:

According to the grace of God which was given to me, like a wise master builder, I laid a foundation and another is building on it. But each man must be careful how he builds on it. For no man can lay a foundation other than the one which is laid, which is Jesus Christ.

(I Cor. 3:10, 11)

He went on to say,

Now if any man builds on the foundation with gold, silver, precious stones, wood, hay, straw, each man's work will become evident; for the day will show it because it is revealed with fire, and the fire itself will test the quality of each man's work. If any man's work which he has built on it remains, he will receive a reward. If any man's work is burned up, he will suffer loss; but he himself will be saved, yet so as through fire.

(I Cor. 3:12-15)

What are gold, silver, and precious stones? These are things that are rare, weighty, and costly. What about wood, hay, and straw? These items are common, ordinary, abundant, cheap, and easily accessible. Paul also told the Corinthians that he determined to know nothing among them except Christ and him crucified (I Corinthians 2:2). His ministry to them was Christ. He ministered to them about what he knew of Christ; what Christ had revealed to him; what Christ had accomplished in his own life; words and messages given to him by the living Lord who was alive in his spirit. Paul's was a ministry of life. It was a ministry based on abiding in Christ, and out of that abiding, sharing with others based on his intimate relationship with the Lord. This is

> *Paul's was a ministry of life. It was a ministry based on abiding in Christ, and out of that abiding, sharing with others based on his intimate relationship with the Lord. This is a rare, weighty, and costly kind of ministry.*

a rare, weighty, and costly kind of ministry. The house of God is built on Christ, not on rules, rituals, good ideas, or humanitarian practices derived from philosophy, human reasoning, and accessible to all men—spiritual or unspiritual alike.

When the remnant first returned to Jerusalem, the first order of business was to clear the building site. After being away for 70 years there was rubble and overgrowth everywhere. They needed to pull up all the weeds, plants, and excess growth, and haul away all the useless clutter. With that out of the way, they were ready to begin.

GATHERED TOGETHER AS ONE MAN

Ezra chapter three begins with the verse: "*And when the seventh month had come, and the children of Israel were in the cities, the people gathered together as one man to Jerusalem.*" Before any work was initiated, the remnant came together as one man in the seventh month. Why the seventh month? It was to remind them of what had caused them to be sent away as captives to Babylon in the first place. They had neglected to observe the Sabbatical year every seven years. They had refused to rest and trust God for his provision. So before they began even the slightest undertaking, God wanted to remind them that everything begins by resting in him.

Not only did they gather together in the seventh month, but they gathered together "*as one man.*" What is the significance of this?

There is a counterpart to this verse in the New Testament. Romans 12:1 says, "*Therefore I urge you, brethren, by the mercies of God to present your bodies a living and holy sacrifice acceptable to God, which is your spiritual service of worship.*"

This is a pivotal verse in the book of Romans. Prior to chapter 12, Paul laid out possibly the most classic, systematic defense of the Christian faith ever written. He wrote about how:

- We are justified by faith.
- Faith leads to peace with God.
- We are saved by his life.
- We have died to sin.
- We have been buried with Christ.
- We have been raised with him and are alive to God and united with Christ.
- We can be delivered from the bondage of our flesh through the power and the life of the Spirit within us.
- We have not only been called and justified, but glorified.
- God has taken care of everything for us.

On top of all this, he wrote about the fact that there is no distinction between Greek and Jew and that God abounds in riches to all who call upon him. Having covered all of these things, he came to chapter 12 verse one, where the whole letter pivots on the word "therefore."

Considering all these things that God had done, all that Paul had written to them about in the previous 11 chapters, and because of God's great goodness and mercies, Paul summed it all up by saying *therefore* it was their spiritual service of worship to present their *bodies* [plural] *a* [singular] living and holy sacrifice to God.

This passage does not say "present your *bodies* as *living sacrifices*," as it is most often quoted. Here Paul said *many* bodies, but only *one* sacrifice. He urged the Roman Christians to come together as *one man* and present themselves as *one body* to God so that God could have a corporate expression of his church in Rome and build his house among them. Following Romans 12:1 Paul went on to talk about the church and our lives as Christians in the body of Christ:

> *For just as we have many members in one body and all the members do not have the same function, so we, who are many, are one body Christ, and individually members one of another. Since we have gifts that differ according to the grace given to us, each of us is to exercise them accordingly; if prophecy, according to the proportion of faith; if service, in his serving, or he who teaches, in his teaching; or he who exhorts, in his exhortation; he who gives, with liberality; he who leads, with diligence; he who shows mercy, with cheerfulness. Let love be without hypocrisy. Abhor what is evil; cling to what is good. Be devoted to one another in brotherly love; give preference to one another in honor; not lagging behind in diligence, fervent in spirit, serving the Lord; rejoicing in hope, persevering in tribulation, devoted to prayer, contributing to the needs of the saints, practicing hospitality...*
> (Rom. 12:4-13)

There is an aspect of Christianity that is individual. Individual consecration to God is essential. But there is also an aspect of Christianity that is corporate. A corporate consecration to the plan and purpose of God is also essential, but rare.

God wants to express himself through a *body*. That *body* needs to be built up together into *one man,*

There is an aspect of Christianity that is individual. Individual consecration to God is essential. But there is also an aspect of Christianity that is corporate. A corporate consecration to the plan and purpose of God is also essential, but rare.

or as the New Testament calls it, *"the new man"* (Eph. 2:15 and 4:24). To do that, God needs a group of people who are willing to lay down their lives, their individual agendas, come together as *one man*, and give themselves to God, so that he can have what his heart desires.

Back in the book of Ezra, the remnant that had gathered together in the seventh month as one man were expressing to God that they had left the individualism of the synagogues of Babylon behind them. They had joined forces and returned to Jerusalem to present themselves to God as one body, so that God could restore his temple.

The First Thing Restored Was the Altar

Following presenting themselves as one man to God, the people arose and built the altar, *"Now in the seventh month...Jeshua and Zerubbabel and his brothers arose and built the altar" (Ezra 3:2).* Restoration of the temple begins by resting in Christ and erecting the altar.

What does the altar represent? The altar was the place of sacrifice. In John 14:6 Jesus said, *"I am the way, the truth and the life; no man comes to the Father but through Me."* In the Old Testament, the way to the Father began at the altar. In the New Testament, the way to the Father begins at the cross. Spiritually speaking, the remnant returned to the original foundation (Christ), gave themselves to the Lord together as one body, and began to understand something of the finished work of Christ on the cross. This is where God's restoration of building a group of people together begins.

THEY OFFERED BURNT OFFERINGS MORNING AND EVENING

Ezra 3:3 says that once they set up the altar on its foundation, *"they offered burnt offerings on it, to the Lord, both the morning and evening burnt offerings."*

Dating back to the time of Moses in the Old Testament we can find several different kinds of sacrifices or offerings that God required. There was the sin offering, the trespass offering, the peace offering, the meal or grain offering, and the burnt offering. Why did the remnant continue to offer up burnt offerings and not any of the other offerings?

The distinction of the burnt offering is that it was completely consumed on the altar and burnt to ashes. With the other sacrifices, after the animal was killed, the priests were to eat the meat. The offering became their food. In these sacrifices, there was satisfaction for both God and man. But with the burnt offering there was nothing left over for man. That sacrifice was totally for God.

By continually offering the burnt offering morning and evening, the people were saying to God, "We, as one people, offer ourselves to you as a burnt offering. We are completely for you, for your satisfaction, and for your purposes. We give ourselves to you so that you can have a house; so that you can have a temple; and so that you can dwell on earth with man and express yourself, your purpose, and your will among us."

This is how the remnant began once they returned. Any group of people who feel called to see the church restored to what it was intended to be ought to take notice of the hearts of these Old Testament saints and be humbly impressed by their high and holy beginning.

THEY CELEBRATED THE FEAST OF BOOTHS

In addition to offering up the burnt offerings, in Ezra 3:4 it says that they celebrated the Feast of Booths. Historically, there were three main feasts the Jews celebrated each year: The Passover, the Harvest Feast, and the Feast of Booths, or Tabernacles. The Feast of Booths lasted seven days and took place at the height of the seventh month, five days after the Day of Atonement.

The Day of Atonement was the one day of the year that a sacrifice was made for the sins of all the people. The blood was brought into the Holy of Holies and presented before God, and all the sins the people had committed during the previous year were covered or atoned. After the atoning sacrifice, all of Israel was considered clean. If there was ever any time of year they felt free and could rest, it was during this time. The remnant must have had an awareness of much of this spiritual legacy that they had not been able to celebrate together as a people for 70 years.

It is interesting to note, however, that as they celebrated the Feast of Booths, it must not have been a complete celebration, but only a partial celebration. Apparently they celebrated the "feast" portion, but they neglected the aspect of actually going out and erecting temporary shelters made from living palm and willow branches and living in booths for a week (as they did when this feast was originally celebrated). We learn this by reading ahead in Nehemiah 8:17, where the people once again celebrated the feast, but this time they celebrated the complete feast by constructing and living in booths, something that the Jews had not done since the days of Joshua the son of Nun.

Later, we'll look more closely at the significance of this celebration when we get to the book of Nehemiah. But for now, what spiritual lesson can we learn from this segment of the story?

We know that the people must have had at least a partial understanding of what this celebration represented. Their partial understanding of this feast reminds me of a conversation I had as a very young Christian with a man I considered to have great spiritual depth and maturity. While sitting in a Chinese restaurant enjoying a good bowl of noodle soup together, he explained to me that there are many truths that we learn in our Christian lives. Every now and then, however, God will bring us back again to rediscover an old truth that we've learned before, only this time we'll see it in a much fuller way.

I can think of an example of this when I first discovered the love of God. I recall the day I asked Jesus into my heart and realized that God so loved the world that he sent his only begotten Son for me. I repented of my sins, received forgiveness, and became a child of God. I knew and had the assurance that all of my sins had been forgiven and that I was heaven bound. This is when I first tasted of his love.

As I began to grow in Christ and gain more experience as a Christian I recall having subsequent revelations that deepened my understanding of his love. The next revelation I remember having was that God didn't love me because I was such a great guy or because of what I had to offer him. He loved me just because he loved me.

This truth is beautifully stated in Deuteronomy 7:6-8 where the Lord said to Israel,

> *"For you are a holy people to the Lord your God; the Lord your God has chosen you to be a people for His own possession out of all the peoples who are on the face of the earth. The Lord did*

not set His love on you nor choose you because you were more in number than any of the peoples, for you were the fewest of all peoples, but because the Lord loved you…"

There was nothing I could do—no works of righteousness, no excessive devotion—to earn more of his love. He loved me because he loved me. It was all because of his grace.

Another revelation came as I began to understand the depth of my sin nature and how God loved me, even in spite of that. It was not just a matter that I sinned every once in a while, it was the realization that I was a sin factory! Sin lived in me (Romans 7:20, 21). Were it not for the grace of God and his Spirit living in me, I'd be sinning all the time and God knows that. Yet, in spite of that, he still loves me!

It was not that I hadn't known the love of God before. It was that now I had begun to understand some of the depths of that love. God brought me back to something I had seen before, and only partially understood, but now with more experience and perspective, I could appreciate that truth in a much fuller way.

THE FOUNDATION LAID AND WORSHIP RESTORED

After two years they finally had something to show for their work. The altar had been set up, the foundation had been laid, and this resulted in immense worship. The people praised the Lord, sang, shouted, and expressed great joy.

Now when the builders had laid the foundation of the temple of the Lord, the priests stood in their apparel with trumpets, and

the Levites, the sons of Asaph, with cymbals, to praise the Lord
according to the directions of King David of Israel. They sang,
praising and giving thanks to the Lord, saying, "For He is good,
for His lovingkindness is upon Israel forever." And all the people
shouted with a great shout when they praised the Lord because
the foundation of the house of the Lord was laid. Yet many of the
priests and Levites and heads of fathers' households, the old men
who had seen the first temple, wept with a loud voice when the
foundation of this house was laid before their eyes, while many
shouted aloud for joy, so that the people could not distinguish the
sound of the shout of joy from the sound of the weeping of the
people, for the people shouted with a loud shout, and the sound
was heard far away.

(Ezra 3:10-13)

By this point in God's recovery we see that the remnant had heard and responded to his call to return to Jerusalem. They experienced the freedom and joy that comes with leaving the land of confusion and false religion, and returning to the city of peace. They began to build on the original foundation and came together as one man. They restored the altar, symbolizing a return to the cross and knowing something of the finished work of Christ. They offered themselves to the Lord as a living sacrifice and burnt offering. They began to experience something of living "in Christ" as represented by the celebration of the Feast of Booths. As a result of all this, God's house was in the beginning stages of being rebuilt according to the original pattern and after two years of hard work, worship was restored.

I've seen many groups of people come together to start a new church. Some get started pretty well. Often there is a great sense of joy as people experience being able to worship freely in a corporate way. Restoring worship is one of the first, and relatively easiest, things to be restored. But at this stage, as we see from the example in the book of Ezra, God had only begun to restore his house. There was much more to accomplish.

> *Restoring worship is one of the first, and relatively easiest, things to be restored. But at this stage, as we see from the example in the book of Ezra, God had only begun to restore his house.*

As we come to the close of Ezra chapter three, the people came together to celebrate and praise the Lord because the foundation had been completed. This resulted in a loud sound coming from Jerusalem. It was a mixture of shouting, joy, and weeping. The young people shouted for joy. But the older ones, who were probably 80 or 90 years old because they had seen the former temple, wept.

People can weep because they're happy or weep because they're sad. Sometimes they can weep because they are both happy and sad at the same time. Regardless, with the return of the remnant and completion of the altar and the foundation, this marks the end of the first revival in the book of Ezra. From here the story takes a turn and the work comes to an abrupt stop. In the next chapter, we'll explore the reasons for this and then see God's remedy to bring them back to the work.

Chapter Six

WHAT'S INSIDE THE DEVIL'S TOOLBOX?
THE WORK STOPS—HAGGAI'S MESSAGE

Then the people of the land <u>discouraged</u> the people of Judah, and <u>frightened</u> them from building, and hired counselors against them to <u>frustrate</u> their counsel all the days of Cyrus king of Persia, even until the reign of Darius king of Persia. Now in the reign of Ahasuerus, in the beginning of his reign, they wrote an <u>accusation</u> against the inhabitants of Judah and Jerusalem.

(Ezra 4: 4-6)

Then as soon as the copy of King Artaxerxes' document was read before Rehum and Shimshai the scribe and their colleagues, they went in haste to Jerusalem to the Jews and stopped them by force of arms. Then work on the house of God in Jerusalem ceased, and it was stopped until the second year of the reign of Darius king of Persia.

(Ezra 4:23, 24)

Following King Cyrus of Persia, his son ascended to the throne. He was followed by Darius. Darius began his reign in about 521 B.C.

In 536 B.C. the remnant returned to Jerusalem to begin the work. They finished the altar and the foundation in two years. Then for 15-16 years the building work on the temple came to a halt. Spiritually, there was no building, no going forward, no growth or progress in the people's relationship with God, and no cooperation with his purpose. In 520 B.C. the work on the temple resumed once again and by 516 B.C. the temple was completed. What was responsible for the people going back to work after being in such a spiritual coma for all those years? They needed another revival. They needed to be brought back to life again. A half-completed temple was no honor to the Lord.

We learn from the book of Haggai that it was in the second year of the reign of Darius (520 B.C.) that the word of the Lord came to Haggai and he prophesied to the people. Two months later the word of the Lord came to Zechariah, and he prophesied as well.

For all those years the work on the temple had ceased. But then when God raised up the prophets to bring the word of the Lord and fresh vision to the people, they were revived and returned to complete what God had called them to do. It was God who took the initiative. He is the Alpha and Omega, the beginning and the end.

The following verses provide a time sequence for these events.

"In the second year of Darius the king, on the first day of the sixth month, the word of the Lord came by the prophet Haggai to Zerubbabel the son of Shealtiel, governor of Judah, and to Joshua the son of Jehozadak, the high priest, saying, 'Thus says the Lord of hosts, "This people says, 'The time has not come, even the time for the house of the Lord to be rebuilt.'"' Then the word of the Lord came by Haggai the prophet, saying..."

(Hag. 1:1-3)

In the eighth month of the second year of Darius, the word of the Lord came to Zechariah the prophet, the son of Berechiah, the son of Iddo saying...

(Zech. 1:1)

When the prophets, Haggai the prophet and Zechariah the son of Iddo, prophesied to the Jews who were in Judah and Jerusalem in the name of the God of Israel, who was over them, then Zerubbabel the son of Shealtiel and Jeshua the son of Jozadak arose and began to rebuild the house of God which is in Jerusalem: and the prophets of God were with them and supporting them.

(Ezra 5: 1, 2)

And the elders of the Jews were successful in building through the prophesying of Haggai the prophet and Zechariah the son of Iddo. And they finished building according to the command of the God of Israel and the decree of Cyrus, Darius, and Artaxerxes king of Persia. This temple was completed on the third day of the month Adar; it was the sixth year of the reign of Darius. And the sons of Israel, the priests, the Levites and the rest of the exiles, celebrated the dedication of this house of God with joy.

(Ezra 6:14-16)

THE REBUILDERS VERSUS THE DISCOURAGERS

The restoration of the temple was going fine until the remnant began to have some problems with the local people of the land. These were Samaritans.

In a previous exile, Israel was carried away from their own land into Assyria (II Kings 17:22-29) and the king of Assyria sent people from Babylon and elsewhere to settle the cities of Samaria. Later, a priest from the exile was sent back to teach them, but it says that the nations still made gods of their own and put them in the houses of the high places where they worshipped (verse 29).

It was the descendants of these Samaritans who came to the Jews and told them that they wanted to help build the temple. But they didn't tell the whole truth. They said, *"Let us build with you, for we, like you, seek your God" (Ezra 4:2)*. They may have said that they sought the God of the Jews, but they still practiced infant sacrifice and many other wicked things. This is where the grudge between the Samaritans and the Jews began and it continued into New Testament times as we read about in the stories of the woman at the well (John chapter four) and the Good Samaritan (Luke chapter ten).

Being unsuccessful at getting invited to build the temple along with the remnant, the locals turned against them and successfully got them to stop building. The four reasons given for why the people stopped building are spelled out in Ezra 4:4-6: discouragement, fear, frustration, and accusations.

Relating this to the world we live in today, it would be as if the local government officials came to a church and said, "You can't meet together or praise the Lord together anymore." In response, some could take the position that as good Christians, the right thing to do would be to obey the government authorities, submit to their demands, and continue worshipping together again at some future date when the time was right. As the Scripture says,

> *Every person is to be in subjection to the governing authorities. For there is no authority except from God, and those which exist are established by God. Therefore whoever resists authority has opposed the ordinance of God; and they who have opposed will receive condemnation upon themselves.*
>
> (Rom. 13:1, 2)

Others may argue, when faced by such an unreasonable request and one that clearly went against the will of God, that the local government's demands should be ignored. We see precedent for this when Peter and John were arrested, put in jail, and then interrogated and chastened by the rulers, the elders, the scribes, and the high priest. Their response, when told that they could no longer speak to any man in the name of Christ, was, *"Whether it is right in the sight of God to give heed to you rather than to God, you be the judge; for we cannot stop speaking about what we have seen and heard"* (Acts 4: 19-20).

We don't know what the local Samaritans told the people, but we do know that they were persuasive enough to cause them walk away from the work on the temple and cease their forward progress with the Lord. We know that the people were discouraged, fearful, frustrated, and accused. Do these "tools" their enemies used look familiar to you? Aren't these the same tools that the enemy of our souls uses against us today? Isn't this just like holding a mirror up in front of our own faces? Haven't we all at one time or another succumbed to these same voices and whispers in our minds that make us doubt that God is really with us and make us want to quit and throw in the towel?

> *We know that the people were discouraged, fearful, frustrated, and accused. Do these "tools" their enemies used look familiar to you? Aren't these the same tools that the enemy of our souls uses against us today?*

THE FIFTH FACTOR

The local opposition also wrote a letter to King Artaxerxes telling him lies about the people and what they were doing. When they received back word from the king affirming their position that indeed the work must stop, they quickly rounded up a group of armed thugs, returned to the building site, and stopped them from building "by force of arms" (Ezra 4:23). God's people were already discouraged, frightened, frustrated, and accused, but now their lives were threatened. This was the final nail in the coffin. This brought the work to a complete stop.

WHAT IS THE LESSON HERE FOR US?

In Acts chapter eight we read where Saul persecuted the church in Jerusalem and the people were scattered throughout the regions of Judea and Samaria. Throughout history and up until this very hour, God has used persecution not only to change the course of his work and bring the gospel to new areas, but also to purify his church and cause it to flourish and grow. (There are, however, exceptions. For instance, in North Africa and large portions of the Middle East where Christianity once thrived, persecution became so severe under the Muslim rampage of "convert, pay tribute, or die" that it was almost completely wiped out and until recently, has remained in that condition for centuries.)

In some places throughout the world the church lives under constant threat of persecution. In other places it does not. Regardless, there is a universal, spiritual application pictured in Ezra 4:23 applicable to believers everywhere. Those Jews did not want to die or be harmed so they stopped building. Human nature seeks to avoid death at all cost—both physical death *and* death to our own selfish interests. The spiritual application we can take from this passage and apply to our own lives is that following Jesus requires willingness on our part to go to the cross and die to self or we cannot be his disciples. Let's see what Jesus and the apostle Paul said about this in the New Testament.

Immediately following Peter's life-altering revelation in Matthew 16:16 that Jesus was the Christ, the Son of the living God, Matthew went on to say that:

> *From that time Jesus began to show His disciples that He must go to Jerusalem, and suffer many things from the elders and chief priests and scribes, and be killed, and be raised up on the third day. Peter took Him aside and began to rebuke Him, saying, "God forbid it, Lord! This shall never happen to You." But He turned and said to Peter, "Get behind Me, Satan! You are a stumbling block to Me; for you are not setting your mind on God's interests, but man's." Then Jesus said to his disciples, "If anyone wishes to come after Me, he must deny himself, and take up his cross and follow Me. For whoever wishes to save his life will lose it; but whoever loses his life for My sake will find it."*
>
> (Matthew 16:21-25)

"God forbid it, <u>Lord</u>!" Those famous, contradictory words spoken by Simon Peter 2,000 years ago have been preserved in the Scriptures to help give us a window into our own hearts. How can anyone call Jesus their Lord and Master and in the same breath tell him that he is wrong? Yet, like Peter, don't we sometimes call Jesus "our Lord," while at the same time, refuse to accept what he is asking of us? And at that point of refusal, doesn't the issue often have to do with our not being willing to take up our own crosses and follow him?

Human nature sees Jesus going to the cross as foolishness, and sees ourselves going to the cross as even greater foolishness! But if Jesus could have been persuaded not to go to the cross, the Devil would have ultimately been victorious. Had Christ not gone to the cross, there would have been no redemption, no resurrection, no life, and no salvation for mankind. No wonder Jesus issued that harsh statement to Peter, *"Get behind Me, Satan!"*

If we are to follow in Jesus' footsteps, like the remnant, we not only need to learn to resist giving in to things like discouragement, fear, frustration, and accusations, but we also need to learn the lesson of being willing to go to the cross. Jesus told his disciples that they must deny themselves and take up their crosses *daily* and follow him (Luke 9:23). Without the work of the cross in our lives, God's transforming work in us cannot go forward, we will have no life to give others, and the body of Christ will not be built up and brought to maturity.

> *Without the work of the cross in our lives, God's transforming work in us cannot go forward, we will have no life to give others, and the body of Christ will not be built up and brought to maturity.*

In II Corinthians 4:7-12 Paul wrote about cross bearing. He said that *"we have this treasure [Christ] in earthen vessels"* but that in order for this treasure to be released in and through us, we need to embrace the cross:

> *...always carrying about in the body the dying of Jesus, so that the life of Jesus also may be manifested in our body. For we who live are constantly being delivered over to death for Jesus' sake, so that the life of Jesus also may be manifested in our mortal flesh. So death works in us, but life in you.*
>
> (II Cor. 4:10-12)

What does it mean for us to take up our cross and follow Jesus? When God brings the cross into our lives it comes in different shapes and sizes and can last for various durations. But in the simplest terms, taking up our cross means dying to ourselves and placing God's interests above our own. It means choosing to live by his Spirit and life within us versus living by our own fallen human nature. The purpose of the cross is to replace something in us with something of God.

Applying this principle to a circumstance we might encounter in daily life, let's think about how we may react to someone who says something very negative about us or may even want to harm us.

In the book of James it says that *"we all stumble in many ways. If anyone does not stumble in what he says, he is a perfect man..."* *(James 3:2)*. It goes on to say that though the tongue is a small part of the body it can do great damage. It is like a small fire that can set a whole forest aflame. With the tongue men boast and curse other men. James 3:8-10 says,

> *But no one can tame the tongue; it is a restless evil and full of deadly poison. With it we bless our Lord and Father, and with it we curse men, who have been made in the likeness of God; from the same mouth come both blessing and cursing. My brethren, these things ought not to be this way.*

At one time or another, we've all undoubtedly had someone speak evil of us, or falsely accuse, slander, or misrepresent us. In those situations, what should be our response? When speaking of them (or to them) what should we allow to come forth from that wiggly, little, red muscle inside our mouths?

Our natural reaction in such circumstances is to lash out, to return fire with fire, and to defend ourselves. But what was Jesus' reaction when he stood before Pilate having been mocked, falsely accused, humiliated, lied about, spat upon, beaten, and whipped? Did he retaliate? Did he respond to each of the false charges? No. He held his tongue. His tongue was crucified before his hands and feet ever accepted the nails.

Christ is our example. He is our standard bearer. Jesus demonstrated how divine life responds when under attack.

In theory, holding back from speaking evil about another person may not always sound like such a difficult thing to do. But when you're feeling angry and caught

But what was Jesus' reaction when he stood before Pilate having been mocked, falsely accused, humiliated, lied about, spat upon, beaten, and whipped? Did he retaliate? Did he respond to each of the false charges? No. He held his tongue. His tongue was crucified before his hands and feet ever accepted the nails.

up in the emotion of a misunderstanding or an argument, it can be a raging battle of epic proportions to keep from going negative.

The next time that you get hurt by something someone says about you and in the heat of the moment feel justified cursing or saying just about anything under the sun that could be said about that other human being, what are you going to do? When those ugly, hateful words begin to form on your tongue and their intensity magnifies by the millisecond, will you let them fly, or will you choose to do something else? There is another option. You can choose to go to the cross.

Sometimes the experience of the cross, momentary or prolonged as it may be, can seem as painful and agonizing to us as enduring a physical crucifixion. Nonetheless, we have been called to follow in the footsteps of Christ.

For the Jewish remnant, the principle of being willing to go to the cross and "die" to their selfish interests was something they still needed to learn. They had stopped going forward with the Lord and needed some kind of divine intervention. Praise God that he did not leave them to themselves. There was a cure for their situation. God sent his two prophets Haggai and Zechariah with a word for the people that got them going again.

The discouragement, the frustration, the accusations, and so forth, to be sure, contributed to why they had stopped building. But it was the revelation given to Haggai and Zechariah that shed light on the real reasons behind why they quit. For us to understand what was really happening beneath the surface in the people's hearts, we need insight into what these prophets had to say. May God help us by giving us these insights, so that when we find ourselves in similar situations, we'll know the way out.

WHO WERE THESE PROPHETS?

Haggai was either born in captivity or taken away from Jerusalem to Babylon at an early age. Haggai is the old prophet. Zechariah 2:4 tells us that Zechariah was the young prophet. God used an old man and a young man to get his people back on track.

The book of Haggai is very short. It covers only four months and is only two chapters long. Haggai was blunt, hard-hitting, and to the point. He spoke with conviction. Zechariah, the younger prophet, took 14 chapters to say what he needed to say. His message was filled with encouragement and comfort. If you are in a spiritual coma, you need both a Haggai and a Zechariah. You need to be convicted and you also need to be encouraged.

HAGGAI'S MESSAGE

Thus says the Lord of hosts, "This people say, 'The time has not come, even the time for the house of the Lord to be rebuilt.'" Then the word of the Lord came by Haggai the prophet, saying, "Is it time for you yourselves to dwell in your paneled houses while this house lies desolate?" Now therefore, thus says the Lord of hosts, "Consider your ways! You have sown much, but harvest little; you eat, but there is not enough to be satisfied; you drink, but there is not enough to become drunk; you put on clothing, but no one is warm enough; and he who earns, earns wages to put into a purse with holes." Thus says the Lord of hosts, "Consider your ways! Go up to the mountains, bring wood and rebuild the temple, that I may be pleased with it and be glorified," says the Lord. "You look for much, but behold, it comes to little; when you bring it home, I blow it away. Why?" declares the Lord of hosts, "Because of My house which lies desolate, while each of you runs to his own house. Therefore, because of you the sky has withheld its dew and the earth has withheld its produce. I called for a drought on the land, on the mountains, on the grain, on the new wine, on the oil, on what the ground produces, on men, on cattle, and on all the labor of your hands." Then Zerubbabel the son of Shealtiel, and Joshua the son of Jehozadak, the high priest, with all the remnant of the people, obeyed the voice of the Lord their God and the words of Haggai the prophet, as the Lord their God had sent him. And the people showed reverence for the Lord. Then Haggai, the messenger of the Lord, spoke by the commission of the Lord to the people saying, "I am with you," declares the Lord. So the Lord stirred up the spirit of Zerubbabel the son of Shealtiel, governor of Judah, and the spirit of Joshua the son of Jehozadak, the high priest, and the spirit of all the remnant of the people; and they came and worked on the house of the Lord of hosts, their God.

(Haggai 1: 2-14)

IT'S NOT TIME

The people said that it was not the time to work on the house of the Lord, but it was time for them to spend on their own paneled houses. They had every intention of following the Lord—someday.

> *They had every intention of following the Lord—someday.*

Their problem was not willful, outright rebellion and sin. Their problem was "self." Their concern had become "my house, my dreams, my plans, my schedule, my time, and my priorities." God's priorities became secondary.

Putting God in second place resulted in a loss of contentment. The people were empty inside and could not find satisfaction in their labors, their clothing, their wages, or their daily provision. You can almost hear them saying, "I have my paneled house, but that's not enough. I have food to eat, but I'd like more. I have wine to drink, but not enough to get drunk. I have clothes and wages, but my money just continues to slip away."

In one sense the past 15 years had been fruitful years. They had what they needed, but still were not satisfied. The Lord brought on a drought by withholding rain and the produce from the land. The people not only experienced a physical drought, but a spiritual drought as well because they lacked the satisfaction and contentment that comes with following the Lord.

THE TASK IS IMPOSSIBLE

Another reason the building stopped was that the people had come to the conclusion that the task God had called them to was utterly impossible. Haggai 1:7, 8 reads, *"Thus says the Lord of hosts, 'Consider your ways!' 'Go up to the mountains, bring wood and rebuild the temple, that I may be pleased with it and be glorified.' says the Lord."*

As we step back and try to put the rebuilding of the temple in perspective by looking at it from the point of view of those who returned, we can easily see that the remnant could have had the overwhelming sense that what God had called them to do was just beyond their capacity to perform. God had not just called them to return to Jerusalem to build a temple, but they were called to rebuild *Solomon's* temple. We read in I Kings chapter five that when Solomon built his temple, it took almost 185,000 laborers seven years to complete it and another 13 years to finish the royal palace and surrounding buildings. That doesn't even take into account all the effort and expense David put into gathering all the materials, drawing up the plans, and getting everything ready before Solomon began.

By contrast, look at the remnant. They were only about 50,000 in number. They had been in captivity. They didn't have the special tools, skills, or experience to do such a work. When they compared what they were doing with the former glory of Solomon's temple and were told "to go up to the mountains and bring wood and build the temple," their reaction was probably, "Yea, right!"

But is it any different today? Doesn't living the Christian life or trying to recover a first-century type church experience sometimes seem just as impossible as the task of rebuilding Solomon's

> *Doesn't living the Christian life or trying to recover a first-century type church experience sometimes seem just as impossible as the task of rebuilding Solomon's temple must have seemed to the remnant, that had a lot fewer people, fewer resources, fewer skills, and enemies all around harassing them and trying to get them to stop?*

temple must have seemed to the remnant, that had a lot fewer people, fewer resources, fewer skills, and enemies all around harassing them and trying to get them to stop?

The fact is that the Christian life is a life that is impossible to live. There is only one person in the universe capable of living it, and that is Jesus Christ himself. Consider these standards of Christian living:

- When your enemy strikes you turn the other cheek.
- Give thanks in all things.
- Be perfect as your father in heaven is perfect.
- Husbands love your wives as Christ loved the church.
- Wives submit to your husbands.
- Be angry, but don't sin.

When people reach the point that they really see that what God is calling them to do is something that is impossible and unattainable, they usually respond in one of two ways. First, they might try harder. Those are the ones who think that if they resolve to pray more, fast more, give more, study more, go to more meetings, or join more committees that they might just be able to do all that God is asking of them. The second choice is to conclude that since what is being required is impossible, why not just stand back and let God do it all? Just quit, give up, and throw in the towel. Many people come to this point and conclude that the Christian life just doesn't work.

In the case of the remnant, many probably concluded that the same God who said, "Let there be light," and there was light, could also say, "Let there be a temple," and there would be a temple! In principle, the second response for what to do in the face of an impossible task is probably closer to the answer than the first, but it can also lead to stagnation or doing nothing, which it did in their case. It took the prophet Zechariah to reveal the principle by which God works in relation to his people and put things in the proper perspective:

> *"This is the word of the Lord to Zerubbabel saying, 'Not by might nor by power, but by My Spirit,' says the Lord of hosts. "What are you great mountain? Before Zerubbabel you will become a plain; and he will bring forth the top stone with shouts of 'Grace, grace to it!' Moreover the word of the Lord came to me, saying: "The hands of Zerubbabel have laid the foundation of this temple; his hands shall also finish it."*
>
> (Zech. 4:6-9)

If we read this carefully we will see that the problem of removing the mountain (the seemingly impossible task of completing and rebuilding the temple) would be accomplished by the Spirit. But immediately after reading that, we see that it would also be accomplished through the *hand* of Zerubbabel. God doesn't expect us to overcome any impossible problem by ourselves. But neither is he going to do it all by himself without our participation. God will work, but he also wants to work with us. God's work is a work *by* his Spirit, *using* our hands.

ANOTHER HINDRANCE TO COMPLETING THE NEW WORK OF GOD: THE PAST WORK OF GOD

> *"Who is left among you who saw this temple in its former glory? And how do you see it now? In comparison with it, is this not in your eyes as nothing?"*
>
> (Haggai 2:3)

When the remnant completed the work on the foundation of the temple there was a loud sound that was heard in the land—a sound of shouting and crying. What did this mean? Were some people happy and others people sad? Were the tears shed tears of joy or tears of sadness? Was it the young people, who were on the front lines of God's work for the first time, the ones who were excited and shouting while the old people, who could remember the former temple in all its beauty, the ones who wept? Was the reason the old ones wept because this temple looked like nothing in comparison to what they remembered from the "good old days?"

From this passage in Haggai we can conclude that those who had seen the former work of God were not impressed by this new work that was underway. Could their lack of enthusiasm and support have dampened the spirits of the young ones? Did they view this new work as "shallow" compared with the "deep" work they were familiar with from the past? We can speculate as to why the elders might have wept:

1. In this new temple, there was no Ark of the Covenant, with its contents (the tablets with the Law, the jar of hidden manna, and Aaron's rod that budded). The ark never returned to Jerusalem after it was ransacked by the Babylonians. All that history lost! That ark, with its mercy seat in the shape of a throne from where the invisible God sat and ruled, would never be part of the temple again. How could their joy be complete without the ark in the temple?

2. When the first temple was completed God dramatically sent lightning from heaven to kindle the fire on the altar. That fire originated from God himself, but not so with this new temple. The supernatural was missing. The old way was better.

3. The former temple was made from huge pre-cut stones mined from underground quarries, chiseled to perfection away from the building site, and then set in place without the sound of a hammer. Not so with the stones of the rebuilt temple. The old people probably said to themselves, "Look what we did this time. We just took any of the stones we found lying around and fit them into place. This temple just isn't as special as the former one."

4. After the Babylonians overran Jerusalem, the Urim and Thummin (the stones on the breastplate of the high priest) were never again found. They were used by the high priest to determine the will of God for the people. When someone went to the high priest with a question, the high priest would inquire of God and if the answer were yes, the stones on the breastplate would glow. But if the answer was no, they would not glow. In this rebuilt temple the people could not come to the priests to receive supernatural answers to their problems.

5. Finally, one of the main reasons the old people probably wept was because of the absence of the shekinah glory cloud. For 900 years the shekinah glory cloud had been with the people. When they dedicated the first temple, it came down out of heaven. But after the Babylonians captured the city and the temple and the captivity began, the cloud left, and it hadn't returned.

It might be fair to ask, were the elders justified in their weeping? It is certainly true that the glory of this temple didn't compare to what it was before. Based on their understanding, they had reason to weep. But then Haggai, speaking for the

Lord, went on to say, *"But now take courage…for I am with you (Haggai 2:4).*

God had a plan. His plan was lofty and glorious, far beyond what could be conceived by the natural man. God had used the temple as a physical picture or illustration of something that was still waiting to be revealed in the future. But the people just didn't understand. Then Haggai ripped back the curtain and unveiled the mystery that had been hidden from their eyes.

> *God had used the temple as a physical picture or illustration of something that was still waiting to be revealed in the future.*

THE DESIRE OF ALL NATIONS

"For thus saith the Lord of hosts; 'Yet once, it is a little while, and I will shake the heavens, and the earth, and the sea, and the dry land; And I will shake all nations, and the desire of all nations shall come: and I will fill this house with glory,' saith the Lord of hosts. 'The silver is mine, and the gold is mine,' saith the Lord of hosts. 'The glory of this latter house shall be greater than of the former,' saith the Lord of hosts: 'and in this place will I give peace,' saith the Lord of hosts."

(Hag. 2:6-9 KJV)

God said that he was going to shake the heavens and the earth—all things physical that could be shaken, and then the Desire of All Nations would come. Then the latter glory would be greater (much greater!) than the former. In this verse, the translators of the King James Version of the Bible got it right: the Desire of All Nations. (The New American Standard's rendition of Haggai 2:7 is: *"I will shake the nations; and they will come with the wealth of all nations, and I will fill this house with glory...*') What was Haggai referring to by the "Desire of All Nations?" He was referring to Jesus Christ. When Christ would come then people would know what real glory is, and his glory would be far greater than the former glory of any temple.

The remnant had been trusting in physical things that could be shaken. They were looking to things that they thought were glory but were not. They were trusting in a physical ark. If God had wanted to save the original ark from disappearing into oblivion, he is God! He could have done that. But he chose not to. When the Desire of All Nations would come, an ark would not be necessary because the Divine Presence would no longer be confined to a box, but would take up residence inside the rib cage of the God-man—Jesus Christ.

The people were trusting in the stone tablets of the Law, but these were also lost. What they didn't see was that God had a better covenant to initiate once Christ came, where the Law would not be written on stone tablets but by the Spirit on the tablets of human hearts.

This rebuilt temple was also not as glorious as the former one because there wasn't all the gold or silver that there was in the former temple. But God was looking to the day when his Son would be revealed in whom all the spiritual blessings and riches in the heavenly places are contained (Eph. 1:3).

This temple was also not as glorious because they didn't see the miracles, the excitement, and the signs and wonders that were present before. But what from this or any era from the past compares with the miracles that Christ performed, and above all, his resurrection from the dead?

This time they didn't have a high priest who could tell the future for them because the Urim and the Thummin were lost. But God could have salvaged those if he had wanted to as well. Instead, he chose not to because he knew that with the coming of the new covenant, ordinary human beings would become temples of the living God and would have the anointing from God dwelling within them (I John 2:27).

The older generation was disappointed by the inferior quality of the stones for the temple. But God was going to do something far greater once the Desire of All Nations would come. We read in I Peter 2:24 that *we* are living stones, being built up as a spiritual house. Living stones, with each individual personality uniquely created to express the glory of the living God, have much more glory than inanimate rocks and stones.

This rebuilt temple was only a picture. God, in his sovereignty, would not let the people put their trust in the physical. He wanted to point them to the Desire of All Nations. Christ would be the glory of the greater temple that was to come, and that greater temple that

> *God, in his sovereignty, would not let the people put their trust in the physical. He wanted to point them to the Desire of All Nations.*

God had in mind from before the foundations of the world was the church.

Finally, when the people saw this, there was revival. They came out of retirement. They awoke from their spiritual coma. They got back on track with God's purpose and began to live again.

The lessons they needed to learn are the same lessons we need to learn today. For those of us living in the church age, we need to be reminded that it's not the doctrines or the teachings, represented by the Law written on stone tablets that are the glory in the church. It's not the signs, the wonders, and the miracles, represented by the fire coming down from heaven. It's not the people, represented by the stones in the temple. It's not some man or spiritual leader who can interpret the will of

God for us, represented by the high priest with his Urim and Thummin. The glory of the church is Christ.

If you, or any group of people seeking the restoration of the house of God, are down, discouraged, afraid, frustrated, accused, or not willing to go to the cross, then you need the same revelation from God that the remnant needed: you need to see the Desire of All Nations once again. If you've been busy with your own house or have thought that now is just not the time to give all for the building of God, then you need a fresh revelation of the glory of Christ. If you think things are impossible and the circumstances you face are too great to overcome, your need is still the same as theirs was: to see Christ yet again. If you have been putting your trust in things other than Christ, or if you are hung up by how small and insignificant the work of God seems to be in your own life or that of the church because it doesn't seem to compare to the work he has accomplished in others, then you still need to see the same thing the remnant needed to see. You need to see Christ once more. You need a brand new touch from him. This will bring revival to your life, to the church, and cause new life to burst forth again.

Chapter Seven

THE SECRET TO STAYING ON TRACK: SEEING CHRIST AGAIN. AND AGAIN. AND AGAIN.
ZECHARIAH'S MESSAGE

What does every lost person need? The answer: They need to see Christ. What does every saved person need? The *same answer:* They also need to see Christ. When we are with a lost person, our conscious awareness should be, "How can I minister Christ to this person in word or deed?" When we are with our brothers and sisters in Christ, it is no different. Whether lost or saved, people need to see Christ.

We begin our Christian life with a revelation of Christ when the Holy Spirit illumines our hearts, convicts us of our sin, and shows us Jesus as our Savior. Peter had been following the Lord for a while when one day he received a revelation and saw who Jesus really was. In Matthew 16:15-16 Jesus asked Peter, *"Who do you say I am?" Simon Peter answered, "You are the Christ, the Son of the living God." And Jesus said to him, "Blessed are you, Simon Barjona, because flesh and blood did not reveal this to you but my Father who is in heaven."* He continued to explain that this revelation of who Christ is would be the rock—the foundation—upon which he would build his church.

We need more than just one revelation of Christ. Our growth as Christians is dependent on further revelations of Christ, as Paul indicated by his prayer in Ephesians 1:15-18:

> *For this reason I too, having heard of the faith in the Lord Jesus which exists among you, and your love for all the saints, do not cease giving thanks for you, while making mention in my prayers; that the God of our Lord Jesus Christ, the Father of glory, may give you a spirit of wisdom and of revelation in the knowledge of him, the eyes of your heart being enlightened, so that you may know what is the hope of His calling, what are the riches of the glory of His inheritance in the saints.*

When we backslide or are discouraged, what do we need? How can we be restored if we have gotten off track? To get back on track we need a fresh revelation of Christ. In Revelation 1:10-11 John wrote, *"I was in the spirit on the Lord's day, and I heard behind me a loud voice like a trumpet saying, 'Write in a book what you see and send it to the seven churches...'"* John was facing one way and heard a voice behind him. He had to turn around to see where the voice was coming from. He needed to see Christ, but the seven churches in Asia also needed to see Christ. John delivered a message from the Lord specifically to each of those churches. Our Christian life begins, continues to grow, and also gets revived each time we see Christ. When we die, our ultimate destiny is to go to be with him, to see him face to face, be made like him, and be with him forever.

> *Our Christian life begins, continues to grow, and also gets revived each time we see Christ.*

We see this same principle in Haggai's message to God's people. The people had started well, but then got distracted and the work came to a halt for 15 years. Then God took the initiative and sent him and Zechariah to speak to the people. Haggai's message challenged the people to think about what they were doing. He exhorted them insistently, five times repeating the phrase, "Consider your ways."

In Haggai 1:8 the words God spoke to the remnant are still applicable to us today. He said, *"Go up to the mountains, bring wood and rebuild the temple that I may be pleased with it and be glorified," says the Lord."* Spiritually speaking, he was saying that to rebuild God's temple, they needed—and *we* need—to go up to a high place, and see the Lord. We need to take a trip to the heavenly places and get revelation, and bring that revelation back down to where we are, and use it to build God's house.

ZECHARIAH'S MESSAGE

On the back of the prophecies and exhortations of Haggai's message came the words of the Lord through Zechariah. Two months after Haggai brought the Lord's word to the people, Zechariah was raised up to prophesy to them as well.

A major theme in Zechariah's message was "return." *"Return to me, declares the Lord of hosts that I may return to you"* (Zechariah 1:3).

While Haggai's words were few, Zechariah's message was lengthy. The book of Zechariah is full of comfort and encouragement. He included many references to the Messiah. He referred to Jesus as The Branch, The Stone with Seven Eyes, The Good Shepherd, and The One whom they pierced.

Zechariah's message was powerful and so effective because he gave the people a real revelation of Christ. This brought revival to their lives. This made them live again and brought them back to work.

Without going into an in-depth study of the book of Zechariah, we will gain insights from highlighting some of the revelations God gave Zechariah, revelations of Christ that the people needed to see. What were they?

VISION ONE: MY HOUSE WILL BE BUILT

The book of Zechariah records seven or eight visions that the Lord showed him. In the first vision, found in Zechariah 1:8-19, God showed Zechariah a man riding on a red horse and standing among the myrtle trees in a ravine along with three other horses behind him.

Who was this man? The man was the Angel of the Lord. *"So they answered the angel of the Lord who was standing among the myrtle trees and said, 'We have patrolled the earth, and behold, all the earth is peaceful and quiet'"* (verse 11). Who was the Angel of the Lord?

The Angel of the Lord, as he appeared in the Old Testament, was none other than Christ himself. He was there among the myrtle trees *in the ravine*—in the low place—symbolizing the place where the people were. He was there with them even in their low spiritual condition. The world may have been at peace and rest, but the problem was that the Persians were in control. That was good news for the Persians, but bad news for God's people.

Then the angel of the Lord spoke to Zechariah and said:

"Thus says the Lord of hosts, 'I am exceedingly jealous for Jerusalem and Zion, but angry with the nations who are at ease.'"

(1:14)

"I will return to Jerusalem with compassion; My house will be built in it."

(1:16)

"Again proclaim, 'My cities will again overflow with prosperity, and the Lord will again comfort Zion and again choose Jerusalem.'"

(1: 17)

The revelation of Christ here is that God had not forgotten Jerusalem. He had not forgotten his people. He was there with them. He saw their situation and promised to intervene. Isn't this the same assurance that all of us long to hear when we feel distant from him and in some spiritual valley? The Lord is with us!

Whether it is restoring one broken life or restoring God's corporate house, we as his people need to hear this word when we are down and need encouragement to keep going forward. *"I will return to Jerusalem with compassion."*

> *God had not forgotten his people. He was there with them. He saw their situation and promised to intervene. Isn't this the same assurance that all of us long to hear when we feel distant from him and in some spiritual valley? The Lord is with us!*

VISION TWO: THE FOUR CRAFTSMEN

God was with his lowly people, but that's not all. The second vision related to the first one, and was brief, being covered in Zechariah 1:20-21. Here he saw four craftsmen whom God would send to overthrow those who had scattered and discouraged God's people.

God is a righteous judge. He is in control and he will judge the world, including those who appear to be in control and who attempt to thwart the Lord's purposes. God's people needed to see not only that the Lord was with them and would act on their behalf, but also that he was righteous and would eventually bring justice.

They needed to trust him and leave this in his hands. When things go wrong, when persecution comes, it's so easy to look at the problem rather than look beyond it to the solution. We need to continue to look to Christ, no matter the circumstances, and leave the matter of judging those who have done wrong in his hands.

VISION THREE: GOD WOULD BE THEIR PROTECTION AND THE GLORY IN THEIR MIDST

The third vision is a surprising one. Zechariah detailed this vision in 2:1-13. When the people first returned to Jerusalem, their natural inclination was to not start by building the temple, but to first build a wall around the city so that enemies could not ransack and attack them at will. Their first thought was about their own safety and protection. It seemed to make sense that they needed something to separate them from the world before they could work on the temple.

That was not a bad idea, but once again, it shows that their first thought was not to look to God for protection, but rather to what they could do for themselves. The Lord's revelation for them was that *he* would be a wall of fire around them (their protection) and the glory in their midst:

"The angel said to Zechariah, 'run speak to the man who is measuring Jerusalem saying: Jerusalem will be inhabited without

*walls because of the multitude of men and cattle within it. For
I,' declares the Lord, 'will be a wall of fire around her, and I will
be the glory in her midst.'"*

(Zech. 2:4, 5)

He also told them, *"he who touches you touches the apple of
his eye." (Zech. 2:8)* and admonished them to *"Sing for joy and
be glad, O daughter of Zion; for behold I am coming and I will
dwell in your midst,"* declares the Lord (Zech. 2:10).

God was saying to them, and is saying to you, "Trust me! I
am with you! I will judge your enemies. I will protect you. Take
your eyes off the obstacles. Sing and rejoice, for I am with you
and will dwell in your midst!"

VISION FOUR: JOSHUA THE HIGH PRIEST

In Old Testament times, the high priest represented the
whole nation of Israel. The fourth vision, found in Zechariah
3:1 to 4:1 was a vision of Joshua, the high priest. Zechariah 3:3
says, *"Now Joshua was clothed with filthy garments and standing
before the angel."* He was standing before the Lord in filthy garment and Satan was accusing him. In this powerful vision we
see that the whole nation, represented by Joshua, was living
under the accusation of the enemy. But the Lord said, *"The
Lord rebuke you Satan."*

In Unger's commentary on this passage, he gets very graphic
in demonstrating what a strong word is used for "filthy." Literally this meant a garment covered with excrement. Not only
was that what the garment looked like, but it was also what it
smelled like! Satan loves to accuse us and call attention not only
of what we look like but smell like before God.

Immediately following that verse, however, the Lord said,
"Remove the filthy garments from him...I have taken your iniquity

away from you and will cloth you with festal robes" (verse 4) and "a clean turban" (verse 5). God didn't just wash Joshua's garments and try to clean him up. He replaced his old garments with soft, eloquent, expensive, beautiful garments and put a turban on his head. In the Old Testament the turban worn by the high priest had an inscription on it that read, "Holiness to the Lord." In the eyes of God, Joshua and the whole nation was completely holy to him.

One reason the remnant had stopped building was because they felt guilty. They knew they had been called to a great work, but they quit. And just as Joshua symbolized God's people Israel, we can look at this group and understand why people today withdraw from their involvement in the church and from going on with the Lord. Isn't one of the major reasons that they feel guilty and unworthy? People in this condition need a fresh revelation of how clean they are in God's eyes. They need to know how thoroughly they have been cleansed.

> *One reason the remnant had stopped building was because they felt guilty. They knew they had been called to a great work, but they quit.*

Perhaps you sometimes think to yourself, "I have lust in my life; I see greed and pride; I have said and done things that hurt my spouse; I can't control my anger; I have secret sins and blasphemous thoughts." Or maybe you sometimes look at other people in the church and think to yourselves, "What hypocrites! Who does that person think he or she is? I know what they are really like."

We are all susceptible to self-condemnation and to criticizing others. In Romans chapter seven, Paul described himself as a man who wanted to do good but who saw a law operating in the members of his body that continued to drag him down into sin.

His bleak conclusion at the end of Romans chapter seven was, *"Oh wretched man that I am. Who will deliver me from this body of death?"* But that opened the door to the glorious statement in Romans 8:1, *"But thanks be to God. There is no condemnation for those who are in Christ Jesus."*

Similarly, in Zechariah 3:7 the Lord says, *"If you will walk in My ways and if you will perform My service, then you will also govern my house and also have charge of My courts, and I will grant you free access among these who are standing here."*

The Lord made this amazing promise to Joshua. It was a promise that he, the one who had accepted the accusations from the enemy that he was clothed in filthy garments, would have free access to God, just like the angels of God that stand before his presence but have never sinned. Not only that, but Joshua was told that he would be restored to a place of responsibility and authority having charge over the Lord's courts. All this was his (and is ours) on the basis of believing in the finished work of Christ and the total forgiveness that he provided for us on the cross.

Zechariah continued, declaring,

> *"Behold, I am going to bring in My servant the Branch. For behold the stone that I have set before Joshua; on one stone are seven eyes. Behold I will engrave an inscription on it, declares the Lord of hosts, and I will remove the iniquity of that land in one day."*
>
> (Zech. 3:8, 9)

Here the Lord of hosts promised that the Messiah would come and remove the iniquity of the land in one day. This was fulfilled when *all* the sins of the world were placed on Christ and were removed in a single day on the cross at Golgotha.

Where we may see our sin, the seven eyes of God, eyes that see perfectly, see us in Christ. When he looks at us or when he sees his church, he sees only holiness. He sees us clothed in festive robes.

So many people stop going on with the Lord because they feel unworthy and filthy. But this revelation of our complete cleansing in Christ can bring us all back to work, as it did with the remnant in Zechariah's day.

I always marvel when I read Paul's opening salutation in his letter to the Corinthians (I Cor. 1:1-3) where he says, *"Paul…to the church…saints by calling."* The word "saints" literally means "holy ones." As we read the rest of Paul's letter to this group of people, however, we see something quite different. We see a group who, when God gave them spiritual gifts, became conceited over them. We see a group of people more interested in signs and wonders or in worldly wisdom, than in knowing Christ himself.

The Corinthian Christians were taking each other to court, tolerating immorality, and being self-centered. They were not spiritual but fleshly—babes in Christ. Yet Paul, God's ambassador, wrote to them and began his letter by telling them who they really were in Christ: God's holy ones.

Astonishingly, when God sees you he looks at you as if you had never sinned. We learn from God's promise to Joshua (and therefore to all the people) that in Christ there is justification and that we

> *Astonishingly, when God sees you he looks at you as if you had never sinned.*

have complete access to him. The word "justified" means just as if you had never sinned. Another way of saying it is that God sees you *in* Christ and looks at you in the same way he looks at his Son, Jesus. Or even better than that, God looks at you as if you were Jesus.

VISION FIVE: NOT BY MIGHT OR BY POWER, BUT BY MY SPIRIT SAYS THE LORD

Restoring the house of God is not a matter of might or power, but of the Lord's Spirit. The people needed to see this vision of Christ. So now we come to the fifth vision of Zechariah,

> *He said to me, "What do you see?" and I said, "I see, and behold, a lampstand all of gold with its bowl on the top of it, and its seven lamps on it with seven sprouts belonging to each of the lamps which are on the top of it; also two olive trees by it, one on the right side of the bowl and the other on its left side." Then I said to the angel who was speaking with me saying, "What are these, my lord?" So the angel who was speaking with me answered and said to me, "Do you not know what these are?" And I said, "No, my lord." Then he said to me, "This is the word of the Lord to Zerubbabel saying, 'Not by might nor by power but by My Spirit' says the Lord of hosts. "What are you, O great mountain? Before Zerubbabel you will become a plain and he will bring forth the top stone with shouts of "Grace, grace to it." Also the word of the Lord came to me, saying, "The hands of Zerubbabel have laid the foundation of this house, and his hands will finish it. Then you will know that the Lord of hosts has sent me to you. For who has despised the day of small things..."*
>
> (Zechariah 4:2-10)

In this passage we find a familiar verse of Scripture, a verse you may have heard put to music and sung as a spiritual chorus, "Not by might, not by power, but by My Spirit says the Lord."

What is the context of this verse? The context is restoring the house of God. Restoring the house of God is a matter of the Lord's Spirit. The people in Zechariah's time needed to see this vision of Christ. So here the Lord revealed to Zechariah a vision of a golden lampstand.

The theme of the golden lampstand occurs frequently in the Bible. Tracing it from beginning to end would take some time, but in summary:

- One thousand years before Zechariah, God gave Moses the vision of the wilderness tabernacle. He told Moses to build something on earth (the tabernacle) after the pattern of something existing in heaven. The tabernacle was a picture of Christ. God opened the heavens and gave Moses a revelation of Christ, and the tabernacle he built on earth was a replica of the real tabernacle he saw in heaven.

- In John 1:14 it says that, "*the Word* [that was in the beginning with God and was God] *became flesh and dwelt among us....*" In Greek, the word used for "dwelt" is "tabernacled." So this verse should more accurately read, as Young's Literal Translation puts it: "*And the Word became flesh, and did tabernacle among us....*" This obviously refers to Christ.

- The apostle John also wrote, "*And I heard a loud voice from the throne saying, 'Behold the tabernacle of God is among men, and He shall dwell among them, and they shall be his people, and God Himself shall be among them.'*" (Rev. 21:3) This verse also refers to Christ as the tabernacle of God. In this context he is the Bridegroom who has come for his Bride (the church).

- Christ has been, is, and always will be the real tabernacle of God. Everything about the tabernacle represented in the Old Testament is a picture that speaks to us about some aspect of Christ or the work of Christ.
- One of the articles in that tabernacle was that lampstand. The lampstand, therefore, pictured something that was "in Christ."
- What is a lampstand for? The only purpose of a lampstand is to hold up and project the light. That light is Christ.
- In Revelation chapter one John had a revelation and wrote it down in a letter to send to the seven churches in Asia. In it he said, *"And I turned to see the voice that was speaking with me. And having turned I saw seven golden lampstands; and in the middle of the lampstands one like a son of man, clothed in a robe reaching to the feet, and girded across his beast with a golden girdle" (Rev. 1:12, 13).* He went on to say, *"As for the mystery of the seven stars which you saw in My right hand and the seven golden lampstands; the seven starts are the angels of the seven churches, and the seven lampstands are the seven churches." (Rev. 1:20)* The lampstand represents the testimony of God. In the Old Testament it was the temple of God; today it is the church.
- In Romans 5:14 we see that Adam was a type or picture of Christ. Just as Adam was put to sleep and a rib was taken from his side to fashion Eve, so Christ had to die (be put to sleep), be resurrected, ascend to the throne, return from the Father, and become the life-giving Spirit, in order for the church to come into existence. Like Eve, who was Adam's life companion, the church was destined to be Christ's bride and life companion for all eternity.

- Ephesians 5:32 also tells us that Adam and Eve were a picture of Christ and the church. So in this picture of Adam and Eve, we see the church was something that was *in* Christ, came *from* Christ, and will return *to* Christ.

In this vision Zechariah presented a golden lampstand for the people to see. This lampstand, like the one Moses made for the tabernacle, was found also in the holy place in the temple. It represented the testimony of God. God's purpose never changes and he never lowers his standards. He has *always* desired a lampstand (the church)—something that was in him and came forth from him—that would hold up the eternal light (Christ) to manifest the multi-faceted wisdom of God and to be a beacon for the entire world to see.

Later, in the Zechariah chapter four passage, after the vision of the golden lampstand, we come to the verse that says, *"Not by might, nor by power, but by my Spirit says the Lord."* How did Zechariah say that this work of restoration of the temple (and in people's lives) would be accomplished? He said that it would not come about by man's hard work, by force, by following a list of rules and regulations, by religious observances, or by keeping the Law, but it would be a work of his Spirit.

This passage goes on to say, *"What are you, o great mountain? Before Zerubbabel you will become a plain; and he will bring forth the top stone with shouts of 'Grace, grace to it!'" (Zechariah 4:7)* The mountain here represents the impossibility of the task of restoring the house of God. Humanly speaking, it could not be done. But by the supply of God's Spirit, that mountain would become a plain, and the building would be finished. The top stone—the final stone—would be laid, and all would know that it was a work of grace.

God never changes, and this same timeless principle applies to us today. A New Testament parallel to this Zechariah passage can be found in Paul's words of encouragement to the Philippian church, *"For I am confident of this very thing, that He who began a good work in you will perfect it until the day of Christ Jesus" (Philippians 1:6).*

For those of you who have given yourselves to see the restoration of the house of God in our day and who may be tempted to be discouraged because you are not seeing much progress, you need the same encouragement. He will finish what he has begun. Jesus promised his disciples in their day that, *"I will build my church and the gates of Hades will not prevail against it" (Matt. 16:18).* He will complete the work, and it will be a work done by his Spirit, and it will be a work of grace.

A LESSON IN SPIRITUAL WARFARE

As I commented earlier, prior to Haggai and Zechariah's prophesies, the Samaritans of the land had succeeded in causing God's people to stop their work on the temple. They had written an accusatory letter against them to King Artaxerxes, one of Cyrus' successors. In Ezra 4:7-16 we read that this letter accused the Jews of rebuilding "the rebellious and evil city" of Jerusalem. They also told King Artaxerxes that if the Jews were allowed to continue, he would not see tributes, customs, and tolls coming from them and his revenues would be damaged.

The king researched the matter and responded with his own decree that the work should indeed stop. God's people buckled without any resistance.

Have you ever asked yourself why the remnant took this arrow from King Artaxerxes without a fight? There is a time to fight, if what the enemy is saying contradicts what God has told you. They had been falsely accused but they were perfectly within their legal rights to continue the work, based on King Cyrus' proclamation only a few years earlier.

Is there a spiritual lesson we can learn here? Yes! When God's anointed king says something and puts it in writing, believe it! Act on it! Fight for it! When the enemy attacks and opposes what the king has said, we must fight back by rejecting his lies and standing with the truth.

> *Is there a spiritual lesson we can learn here? Yes! When God's anointed king says something and puts it in writing, believe it! Act on it!*

We see this in the way Jesus confronted the Devil's temptations in the wilderness. Jesus refuted Satan by quoting Scripture and proclaiming the truth. When he did that, Satan had to flee.

For instance, in the third temptation the Devil took Jesus up on a high mountain and showed him all the kingdoms of the world and said to him, *"All these things I will give You, if You fall down and worship me."* But our Lord's response was, *"Go, Satan! For it is written, 'You shall worship the Lord your God and serve Him only.'"* Next it says, *"Then the devil left Him..."* (Matt. 4:8-13).

After the people had stopped working on the temple, we read in chapter five of Ezra that the prophets Haggai and Zechariah prophesied to them, and work on the temple immediately resumed. But so did the opposition of the enemy. The Samaritans came back at the Jews once again and said, "Hey! Who said you could do this? Who gave you permission to start building again?" [My paraphrase]

This time, however, the people responded differently. Instead of buckling once again, this time they resisted. They told

Tattenai the governor, Shethar-bozenai, his colleagues, and the officials,

> *"We are servants of the God of heaven and earth and are rebuild-*
> *ing the temple that was built many years ago, which a great king*
> *of Israel built and finished...However, in the first year of Cyrus*
> *king of Babylon, King Cyrus issued a decree to rebuild this house*
> *of God."*
>
> (Ezra 5:11, 13)

Reading between the lines you can hear God's people telling the opposition, "We've resumed building and now we intend to finish it. Cyrus told us we could, and that's all the permission we need. If you have a problem with that, go check it out for yourselves. If you want a fight, bring it on."

So another letter was written, this time to King Darius, saying,

> *"Now if it pleases the king, let a search be conducted in the*
> *king's treasure house, which is there in Babylon, if it be that a*
> *decree was issued by King Cyrus to rebuild this house of God at*
> *Jerusalem; and let the king send to us his decision concerning*
> *this matter."*
>
> (Ezra 5:17)

Sure enough, in one of the fortresses in the province of Media, they found a scroll with King Cyrus' proclamation written on it. Tattenai and his friends received a reply from King Darius saying, *"...keep away from there. Leave this work on the house of God alone; let the governor of the Jews and the elders of the Jews rebuild this house of God on its site"* (Ezra 6:6-7). They were also instructed to give the Jews whatever they needed *"daily without fail"* (Ezra 6:9).

So the enemy was driven away and the temple was completed when the people stood their ground, based on what King Cyrus had said and written. The moral of the story for us is that when we come under spiritual attack—when discouragement, fear, frustration, and accusations come—we need to believe what God has said, trust his word, and stand upon his promises.

The people not only believed what the king had said and written, but also they spoke those words to their enemies. When you find yourself locked in spiritual battle, when you are assaulted with negative thoughts and accusations, you can defend yourself by speaking the truth and proclaiming God's own words right back in the face of the enemy, and he will have to retreat. You have Christ, the living Word. You have the Scriptures. God has given you the shield of faith and the sword of the Spirit, which is the word of God.

Fifteen years of down time was a high price to pay for the remnant to learn this valuable lesson. In the same way, the restoration of God's house today is also long overdue. But what a wonderful illustration this is for us to help us see and discover how to fight the good fight of faith, and lay hold of that for which we were laid hold of by Christ Jesus.

Chapter Eight

Making Good Things Better
Ezra's Return to Beautify the House of God

"He has made everything beautiful in its time." So writes Solomon in Ecclesiastes (3:11a NKJV), and it's true. God has always deserved the best and finest, including the rebuilt temple in Jerusalem. Indeed, Ezra returned to Jerusalem to beautify the temple, but it was many years before this beautification actually happened. Why?

We have seen how God used the prophets Haggai and Zechariah to inspire the people and get them back to work on the temple. This was the second period of revival that came during the 100-year period at the close of the Old Testament record. The people saw a fresh vision of Christ and began to grow and go forward again. They completed the temple in just four years, and dedicated it with great joy (Ezra 6:16).

Now we come to Ezra chapter seven. It begins with the phrase, *"Now after these things..."* What things was Ezra referring to? Between the completion of the building of the temple (that took a total of about 20 years), and this phrase, *"Now after these things...* "was a period of 57-58 years. This is where we first encounter Ezra himself in the book of Ezra—nearly 80 years after the remnant had originally returned to rebuild.

Interestingly, the book of Esther was written during this 57-year period. The setting for the book of Esther was back in Persia (Babylon), where the majority of the Jews stayed behind. Esther was a beautiful Jewish woman who married the Persian king. Through her efforts she was able to come before the king and thwart the efforts of a murderous man named Haman, who had come up with a scheme to have all the Jews destroyed.

One conspicuous thing about the book of Esther is that it is the only book in the Bible where the name of God or Jehovah never appears, not even once. We see the activity and the sovereignty of God throughout the book, but curiously, his name is never mentioned. Why?

> *One conspicuous thing about the book of Esther is that it is the only book in the Bible where the name of God or Jehovah never appears, not even once.*

Could it be because this narrative is about the people of God who remained in captivity and never responded to the call of God to go back to Jerusalem to rebuild the temple? Many think so. God loves all his children and the book of Esther shows us that God does not forget his people. He was there with them, working behind the scenes, even while the real work of God and the forward progress of the kingdom was taking place among the remnant. The remnant's hearts and bodies were where God's heart was—back in Jerusalem.

Not only was God's name not mentioned in the book of Esther, but the perilous condition of the people left behind in Babylon led them to the brink of being entirely wiped out.

They were on the verge of total annihilation because they were not where they were supposed to be or doing what they were supposed to do. They were, by and large, living for themselves and not for God.

There are at least two main lessons we can learn from this story. The first and most obvious lesson is that if you love God, you don't want to be left behind by not responding to God's call, as these did in Babylon. You don't want to be one of those with whom God only works behind the scenes; whom he protects and cares for, but in whose lives his name is never mentioned. You don't want to be one of those that live on the brink of annihilation because you are not serving God and are not where you are supposed to be.

The second lesson has to do with what our attitudes should be toward those who stay behind. If by God's grace, you are one of those who has responded to God's call and is following him with all your heart (God knows who you are), what should your attitude be toward other Christians that are not really following God? What about people who have been saved, but appear to have no interest in pursuing him and are just living their lives for themselves? What if you have a longing inside you to help rebuild the house of God today and yet you come across other Christians who have been invited to become part of the rebuilding, but have no interest in becoming involved in it?

Your attitude should reflect God's attitude. As disappointing as these things can be, you should not be judgmental, prideful, comparative, or boastful. They are ultimately God's responsibility. But for God's grace, we would all be in the same place, or even worse—we'd be swinging from a gallows, like Haman did! God still loves his people. Even when they choose not to respond to his call, he is always working behind the scenes, desiring to reveal himself, and hoping they will see and turn back to him.

AFTER THESE THINGS

The temple was completed. The period of Esther had passed when the Jewish nation was rescued and spared. Now, after this span amounting to about 57 or 58 years had come and gone, we come to Ezra 7:6. Here we read that Ezra came up from Babylon to Jerusalem and about 5,000 to 10,000 others came with him.

Ezra was a scribe and a virtuous man, having *"set his heart to study the law of the Lord and to practice it and to teach his statutes and ordinances in Israel" (Ezra 7:10).* King Artaxerxes of Persia had issued a decree to Ezra that *"any of the people of Israel and their priests and the Levies in my kingdom who are willing to go to Jerusalem may go with you" (Ezra 7:13).* Praise God that this king gave those Jews remaining in Babylon a second chance to go back and to get it right.

Why did Artaxerxes issue this decree? It was because he could see God's sovereignty. He saw that there was a God in heaven and he was afraid of God's wrath and judgment, so he let them go back. *"Whatever is commanded by the God of heaven, let it be done with zeal for the house of the God of heaven, so that there will not be wrath against the kingdom of the king and his sons" (Ezra 7:23).*

Ezra's response to this decree was, *"Blessed be the Lord, the God of our fathers, who has put such a thing as this in the king's heart, to adorn the house of the Lord which is in Jerusalem..."* *(Ezra 7:27).*

Ezra returned to Jerusalem to help adorn, or beautify, the house of God and to teach God's word to the people. The king had given Ezra silver and gold and other valuables to take back for the temple so Ezra selected certain leading priests, weighed out all the valuable things, and made a list of all the items. After the people completed the 700-mile trip and arrived in Jerusalem, everything was then brought out and weighed again, just to make sure it was all there.

These people had good hearts. They were accountable and trustworthy with what they had been given and wanted to do what was right. These qualities of good stewardship and financial accountability should always characterize God's people.

But today, in a spiritual sense, there is another lesson we can learn from this story. Our king (Jesus) wants to give his servants (you and me) "silver and gold" to bring to the church and deposit into his people. Things of redemptive value (silver), things reflecting the nature of God (gold), these are the things that God wishes to deposit into us and wants us to deposit into the lives of others. Indeed, *"His divine power has granted to us everything pertaining to life and godliness" (2 Pet. 1:3a)*. Therefore, we must also be responsible for keeping those things entrusted to us by God and conveying them to others, just as Ezra and the leading priests did.

THE CONDITION IN JERUSALEM WHEN EZRA RETURNED

When Ezra and his company returned to Jerusalem, what did they find? The altar had been set up, the foundation laid, the temple had been completed, and sacrifices were again being offered. That was good but the situation was still tenuous and fragile. The walls were still broken down. There was no separation between the people of God and the people of the world. Though they could worship, they were still easy targets and could be influenced and attacked by their enemies.

The temple was a far cry from what it had been originally. When Solomon dedicated the original temple, he offered up

22,000 oxen and 120,000 sheep. But when Zerubbabel's temple was completed they offered up only 100 bulls, 200 rams, 400 lambs, and 12 male goats as a sin offering for all Israel. In every way, Zerubbabel's temple was inferior to Solomon's temple, but that's the way God wanted it. It was a day of small things and God said not to despise the day of small things.

In addition to the wall being in disrepair and the temple being inferior, the city itself had not been built up. In Solomon's day it took seven years to complete the temple. It took another 13 years to complete the royal palace nearby where Solomon sat on his throne and ruled over his kingdom. In the glory days, Jerusalem was not only a place with a temple for worship, but it was also a place with a royal palace where the kings ruled and reigned over the kingdom.

Indeed, going all the way back to Genesis we can see that God's original purpose for man was to have a corporate people who bore his image and ruled with his authority on this earth:

> *Then God said, "Let us make man in our image, according to our likeness; let them have dominion over the fish of the sea, over the birds of the air, and over the cattle, over all the earth and over every creeping thing that creeps on the earth. God created man in His own image, in the image of God He created him; male and female He created them. God blessed them; and God said to them, Be fruitful and multiply, and fill the earth, and subdue it; and rule over the fish of the sea and the over the birds of the sky and over every living thing that moves on the earth.'"*
> (Gen. 1:26-28)

To illustrate this further, the original temple had been situated on Mount Moriah, the same place where centuries before,

Abraham had made that lonely journey with his son Isaac and offered him up as a sacrifice to God. But God spared the boy's life there on Mount Moriah, and provided a lamb as a substitute sacrifice because of Abraham's obedience. So the temple was built on Mount Moriah, while the royal palace, the house of David, was built on nearby Mount Zion.

Mount Moriah was the location for the Holy of Holies, with the Ark of the Covenant. Mount Zion was the location for the throne. On Mount Moriah the priests served. On Mount Zion the kings ruled. On Mount Moriah was the presence of God. On Mount Zion was the authority of God. And so again we see this recurring theme of image and authority. Later on, we see this distinction of the mountains upon which the temple and the palace were situated dispelled and the entire area simply became known as Mount Zion. But still, this is another clear illustration for us of God's unchangeable purpose.

Though the Jews in Ezra's day had rebuilt the temple, they were still under the thumb of the Persian Empire. There was no palace. They still had people ruling over them. The city had not been restored. God's government had not been established. The wall was broken down and failed to provide protection for the people, for the temple, and for all the worship that took place there.

There was far less glory in Jerusalem when Ezra returned than there was during the days of Solomon, even though the temple was completed. But the people had heard from the prophets Haggai and Zechariah and were waiting for the Desire of All Nations, The Branch, and the Good Shepherd to come; and when he came, the glory of the later house would indeed be greater than that of the former.

BEAUTIFYING THE HOUSE OF GOD

When Ezra returned to Jerusalem with his troop, he did so with purpose. He returned with a heart to teach the people the Word of God, to adorn the temple, and strengthen the temple service. God still needs people to do those things and apply these principles in the church today.

God needs those who can teach the word of God to others and reveal Christ to them from the Scriptures. But what does it mean *for us* that Ezra returned to "adorn, or beautify, the temple?"

The spiritual significance for us as we seek to see God's house restored to its former glory is that we need to concern ourselves with strengthening and beautifying the ministries within the church. For example, take the gift of hospitality. God has gifted

But what does it mean for us that Ezra returned to "adorn, or beautify, the temple?" The spiritual significance for us as we seek to see God's house restored to its former glory is that we need to concern ourselves with strengthening and beautifying the ministries within the church.

many people within the church, to one extent or another, with the gift of hospitality. They have hearts to entertain guests and even open up their homes to visiting Christians and strangers. Maybe they are already doing this, but maybe with a little instruction, this ministry could be developed and "beautified."

Let's say a couple comes to your house to stay for a while. You could offer them the couch or a place on the floor to sleep, and tell them that the bathroom is down the hall, and hope for the best. Or, you could offer them the bed in the master bedroom, set out some towels for them, and place a bowl of fruit or some chocolates and bottled water by their bedside. There's a big difference between the two! Simply receiving those guests, on one hand, is quite different from the hospitality of treating them as if Christ himself had walked through your door. The latter takes hospitality to a new level and really beautifies the house of God.

Two other examples of "adorning the house of God" come to mind. I frequently visit a church in one of the poorer republics of Russia, in the Ural Mountain area. This fruitful church of about 3,000 has planted more than 300 churches in and around the Republic of Udmurtia. One of the many ministries that has developed here is a women's ministry.

Imagine yourself as one of the more zealous women in this church, one who loves the Lord and is eager to serve him. You've been studying your Bible and you come across the verse in James that says, *"pure and undefiled religion in the sight of our God and father is this: to visit orphans and widows in their distress, and to keep oneself unstained by the world" (James 1:27).* So the Lord puts on your heart to visit some of the widows and needy women in your area.

You start out by just visiting them, but then your burden for them grows. You start visiting them regularly, and they bare their hearts to you so you can pray for them. You look around their kitchens and see they have little food. On your next visit you bring them some extra bread or some sweets. After that, you bring them each a sweater or a warm coat to help them survive the cold winters because their clothes are old and worn out. Soon you begin doing other things for these women and start getting other sisters from the church involved.

This is how the women's ministry began in this Russian church. Currently they have more than 50 women from the main church regularly involved, and 70 more from their daughter churches. They visit the widows in the cities, towns, and villages, bringing them food bags, usually consisting of some oil, sugar, flour, and a can of condensed milk. They cut their hair, bring them small gifts, and lead them in Bible studies. Now they also hold regular conferences for women where they teach about a woman's relationship with her husband, raising children, and a woman's place in society. This ministry has grown from something very simple to something very practical and beautiful within the church.

Another example from this church is their ministry to orphans and street children. Teams regularly visit kids in orphanages and those living on the streets. They share Jesus with them, bring them food and clothing, try to get them to stop sniffing glue or using drugs, and just spend time becoming their friends and providing them with some good adult role models.

As I mentioned, this is a very poor republic and most people don't have enough money to do a lot of things we take for granted. When the C.S. Lewis movie, *The Chronicles of Narnia,* came out in the theatres in Russia in January 2006, this church took more than 1,000 orphans and street children to see this movie. For most of the kids, this was the first movie they had ever gone to in their lives. For nearly all of them, this was the first time they got to ride in a bus, sit in a cozy chair inside of a movie theatre, and have the opportunity to become mesmerized by watching this wonderful children's classic on the big screen.

For most of them this was perhaps the greatest event in their lives—something they will never forget. In the weeks following the movie, the church did follow-up work with the kids, talking with them about the significance of the characters and the theme of the movie. Many of these kids ended up accepting Christ. Taking advantage of this event made the church even more beautiful in the eyes of the children, the workers at the orphanages, and the community.

In Psalm 45, a song celebrating the King's marriage, it says, *"The King's daughter is all glorious within; Her clothing is interwoven with gold. She will be led to the King in embroidered word..."* (Ps. 45:13, 14). And Revelation 19:7 says, *"Let us rejoice and be glad and give the glory to Him, for the marriage of the Lamb has come and His bride has made herself ready." It was given to her to clothe herself in fine linen, bright and clean; for the fine linen is the righteous acts of the saints."*

From both of these passages we see that the Bride of Christ is clothed in an elegant garment. It's made of embroidered work of fine, white linen. We're told that this fine linen garment is the righteous acts of the saints. Ezra's burden was to beautify the house of God. The examples of what this church is doing are good reminders for us of the Spirit's work today to prepare the church to meet her bridegroom by making her beautiful through the righteous acts she performs. May we aspire to do such works to beautify God's house today.

STAY TUNED...

Ezra and the company with him delivered all the gold, silver, and articles for the temple that they brought with them. Ezra had in his heart to teach the word of God to the people and to beautify the temple. And he was just about to begin his ministry when we come to the last two chapters of the book, chapters nine and ten.

If we ended our study of the rebuilding of the temple and the restoration of the house of God here, we might find it disappointing, because the book of Ezra ends in a very strange way. It ends on a down note. Here is how it ends:

- When Ezra and this second remnant returned, 57-58 years after the temple had been completed, he was told that the people of Israel, the priests, and the Levites had sinned because they had not separated themselves from the peoples of the land and had married foreign wives. The holy race had been compromised. He was also told that it was the leaders—the princes and the rulers—who had been foremost in this unfaithfulness (Ezra 9:1-2).
- Ezra heard this report and was appalled. He tore his robes, and pulled out some of the hair from his head and beard. He fell prostrate before the Lord and poured out his heart on behalf of the people (Ezra 9:3-15).
- When somebody had the good idea that everyone should get rid of their foreign wives and the children born to them, Ezra rose and made the leading priests, the Levites, and all Israel take an oath that they would do this—and they did (Ezra 10:5).
- Then the book of Ezra ends with a list of all the offenders.

What a strange way to end a book! It gives no resolution to the bigger story. That's why we need to also consider the books of Haggai, Zechariah, Nehemiah, and Malachi—in that order—which are also closely linked to the book of Ezra. These books provide the rest of the story for us, a story with more lessons that the people needed to learn, *and that we need to learn*, in order to help us restore God's house today.

Chapter Nine

Issues of Corporate Life in the Church—Spiritual Authority and Unity
The Book of Nehemiah— Rebuilding the Wall

An Insufficient Oath

Ezra's zeal for the house of God and the people of God made him a man of action. He was not a man of anger, but he loved God and was no one to be trifled with if you were living a life of disobedience. At the end of the book of Ezra, the people were guilty of marrying foreign wives and having offspring from these marriages. Spiritually, we see that God's people had become married to the world and were producing worldly fruit.

Ezra saw it in his time, and wanted to rectify this situation. His solution was to take action and put away the foreign wives. Later, however, we read in the books of Nehemiah and Malachi that the same problem continued to plague them so it never completely went away.

We must understand that this remnant was not a collective group of backsliders. These were not the people who had stayed behind in Babylon. These were people who wanted to get things right. They were the equivalent of the Lord's Special Forces.

In Ezra 10:2, 3 we read that while Ezra was praying, making confession, and weeping over this situation, a man named Shecaniah, the son of Jehiel, came to him and said, *"We have been unfaithful to our God and have married foreign women from the peoples of the land; yet now there is hope for Israel in spite of this. So now let us make a covenant with our God to put away all the wives and their children."*

Ezra wasted no time. *"Then Ezra rose and made the leading priests, the Levites and all Israel, take an oath that they would do according to this proposal; so they took the oath" (Ezra 10:5).* The people took an oath and made a covenant with their God to put away all the foreign wives and their children. They had noble intentions. Wanting to be delivered, they took action, but we find that their remedy did not result in solving the problem.

They acted on what seemed to be a reasonable idea, but they still had not yet received a revelation about how to be delivered. This situation is reminiscent of Romans chapter seven, where Paul wrestled with the fact that sin dwelt in his flesh. He knew the requirements of God. He knew the right thing to do, but he couldn't perform it. He learned through painful experience that trying and trying, making vow after vow, wouldn't deliver him from the power of sin that dwelt in his flesh. In Romans 7:24 he wrote, *"Wretched man that I am! Who will set me free from the body of this death?"*

But thank God, Paul finally learned the secret that true deliverance from the flesh and a life of sin came only through the revelation that:

Therefore there is now no condemnation for those who are in Christ Jesus. For the law of the Spirit of life in Christ Jesus has set you free from the law of sin and of death. For what the Law could not do, weak as it was through the flesh, God did: sending

His own Son in the likeness of sinful flesh and as an offering for sin, He condemned sin in the flesh, so that the requirement of the Law might be fulfilled in us, who do not walk according to the flesh but according to the Spirit.

(Rom. 8:1-4)

God fulfills the requirements of the Law for Paul and for all believers by *his Spirit living in us*, as we abide in him. In another of his epistles Paul also wrote, *"walk by the Spirit, and you will not carry out the desire of the flesh" (Gal. 5:16).*

In New Testament terms, the remnant had experienced justification—deliverance from the penalty of sin. But now they were in need of sanctification—deliverance from the power of sin. To be truly sanctified, they needed a wall with gates to ensure proper separation between themselves and the world. In Zechariah God spoke to the remnant through the prophet saying, *"I will be a wall around her (Jerusalem) and the glory in the midst" (Zech. 3:5).* His promise to them was that *he* would be their protection and deliverance.

> *In New Testament terms, the remnant had experienced justification—deliverance from the penalty of sin. But now they were in need of sanctification—deliverance from the power of sin.*

The New Testament gives us further light on what it means to be sanctified. One definition of sanctified is to be set apart. We need to be set apart from the world in our behavior and our attitudes, but we need to see that this is not something separate from Christ. Sanctification comes as we learn to abide *in Christ*, rest in him, and draw from the power of the life of his Spirit dwelling within us. I Corinthians 1:30, 31 says, *"But by his doing you are **in Christ Jesus, who became to us wisdom*** *from God, and **righteousness** and **sanctification**, and **redemption**, so that just as it is written, "Let him who boasts, boast in the Lord."* [Emphasis mine]

Jesus Christ is our sanctification. God will not allow us to boast that because of our oath, or our determination, or the exercise of our will that we have the strength in ourselves to overcome the sin that lives on in us even after we are born again. As you abide in Christ, you will experience sanctification. This is what the remnant still needed to see.

THE BOOK OF NEHEMIAH

Nehemiah had zeal for the house and the people of God, just as Ezra did. Nehemiah lived in the Persian capitol of Susa and was the cupbearer for the king. His job was to make sure no one poisoned the king by his food or drink. When one of Nehemiah's brothers and some men from Judah returned from Jerusalem, Nehemiah questioned them about how the Jewish remnant was getting along. They reported to him that the remnant was in great distress and that the wall of the city was still broken down and the gates burned.

The news sent Nehemiah into great anguish and mourning. He wept over the situation and finally approached the king to ask his permission to return to Jerusalem to assist in the work of restoration. He got the answer he was hoping for from the king. So in about 444 B.C., Nehemiah led a third group back from Babylon to Jerusalem to work on the wall around the city and to remake and hang the gates.

Without a wall of separation between the Jews and the people on the outside, enemies could come and attack them at will and potentially destroy the temple (that is, destroy the worship) that they had worked to restore and recover. Certainly

God had been and would be their wall, their sanctifier, but for practical purposes a wall still needed to be built.

After Nehemiah returned to Jerusalem and inspected the condition of the wall, he rallied the people and challenged them to *"rebuild the wall of Jerusalem so that we will no longer be a reproach" (Nehemiah 2:17).* The people responded, *"'Let us arise and build.'" So they put their hands to the good work" (Neh. 2:18).*

The people worked together. It was a corporate effort. Everyone had a task to perform and a portion of the wall to work on. At times the enemy resorted to all-out war to stop the building process. When one portion of the wall was attacked, others had to drop what they were doing and come to the aid of those under assault, and stand with them to fight back the enemy. They built together and they fought together. Despite danger and opposition, eventually the wall was completed.

Isn't this a striking picture of what the church ought to be? God has gifted each member in his body with gifts for the common good. We all have our assignments and areas of service. But no one in the body can escape coming under attack from the enemy. When those times come, we all need brothers and sisters we can turn to, who will fight alongside us, pray with us, cry with us, grieve with us, share our burdens, encourage and exhort us, and walk together with us through the dark times until we see the Lord appear and give us victory over our enemies. During those difficult but extraordinary times the Lord may draw a few special people into our lives with whom we become knit together and form a strong, deep bond of Christian unity, and sip from the sweet nectar of true brotherly love. We all need to have brothers and sisters like this in our lives. And we all need to *be* brothers and sisters like this for others.

ENEMIES WITHOUT, ENEMIES WITHIN

When the Jews were rebuilding the wall, the temple had already been rebuilt. It was not as glorious as the first temple. God did this deliberately, so that the people would not trust in buildings or in physical things. He wanted them to see that the real glory would arrive when the Desire of All Nations would come. Then the glory of the later house would be greater than that of the former.

He wanted them to see that the real glory would arrive when the Desire of All Nations would come. Then the glory of the later house would be greater than that of the former.

The same principle held true with the wall. The original wall was thick, high, beautiful, and strong. But the rebuilt wall was nothing in comparison to the original wall. Psalm 48:12 says, *"Walk about Zion and go around her; count her towers; consider her ramparts; go through her palaces, that you may tell it to the next generation."* Yet in Nehemiah 4:2-3, the enemies ridiculed this wall the remnant was building saying: *"'Can they revive the stones from the dusty rubble even the burned ones?' Now Tobiah the Ammorite was near him and he said, 'Even what they are building—if a fox should jump on it, he would break their stone wall down!'"* So the rebuilt wall, like the rebuilt temple, was nothing in comparison to the original. But this, too, was by God's design. God did not want his people to put their trust in the physical. He wanted them to trust him to be their protection.

While the Jews were busy building the wall and fighting off the enemies without, another problem came to light. This was a problem from the inside. This problem, found in Nehemiah chapter five, concerned the relationship between the common people and their leaders, the nobles, and the priests. Those who were ruling over the people began extracting money from them and dominating them. Many of the common people were so beaten down by this exploitation that they had to mortgage their lands; they were without food, and they even had to sell their sons and daughters as slaves, while the nobles and the rulers got rich.

When Nehemiah heard this, he became furious. He immediately took action, exhorting the nobles and priests, *"Please, give back to them this very day their fields, their vineyards, their olive groves and their houses, also the hundredth part of the money and of the grain, the new wine and the oil that you are extracting from them" (Neh. 5:11).* In response to Nehemiah's exhortation, the nobles and priests agreed to do what he said.

A Great Obstacle to Real Church Growth and Maturity: The Clergy-laity System

When any group of people attempt to restore the house of God and rebuild on the original foundation, which is Christ, they can do many of the right things, but still be in danger of falling short of the mark. They can restore worship. They can begin to separate themselves from the world and establish a testimony. But in the process, they can also get trapped in one of the greatest pitfalls that groups encounter. The leaders can begin to set themselves apart from the common people and usurp from them what was rightfully theirs.

We see this in the story of Nehemiah. The common people became so indebted to their leaders that the leaders ended up owning everything and the common people owned nothing. We see this today in the clergy-laity system that has developed in most churches, where nearly all the functioning, all the responsibility, all the leadership, all the governing, and all the preaching and teaching has been "usurped" from the common people and is in the hands of a professional clergy.

The majority of the people in churches today have relinquished what God had originally appointed for them. The few have, in a sense, become rich. They have too much. They do too much. They over-function. The masses have become poor. They are poor in regard to being given responsibility to serve and in the blessings that come with serving. In fact, most people in today's churches have almost no responsibility. (Just think, men, if you are one of the privileged few, you'll get to go to church on Sunday and set out the cookies!) Because they have been given little responsibility, they have been hampered from expressing their God-given gifts within the body of Christ.

In an article in *House2House* magazine (issue number 6) entitled, "Where in the World Is the Church?" Tony Dale appropriately comments,

> By concentrating power and authority into the hands of a special or professional class, usually called "clergy," the church has marginalized and thereby rendered ineffective most of its members. How well I remember the frustration of being an experienced professional, leading teams of people in my medical practice, and competent to set up conferences for physicians from all over the country, but apparently not competent enough to teach a Sunday school class at the church. Something is wrong with this picture.

Tony goes on to say,

> We have marginalized the God-given missionary or growth forces within the church and labeled them "para-church." Much of the real impetus for church growth and maturation has come through the so-called "para-church" organizations,

because we tend to force the apostolic and prophetic types out of our churches that prefer a "pastor dominated" form of leadership. The result is vision-depleted churches, tending to the needs of their members, rather than Spirit-inspired assemblies, reaching out to deal with the needs of the world.

Gifted leaders who are trapped within this clergy-laity system often cannot find their place or are not given opportunity to function within the local church. Frequently, the only outlet for them if they are to pursue their gifts and callings, is to leave and start their own church or para-church organization.

PASTOR-DOMINATED, SUNDAY MORNING CHURCH SERVICES, OR INTERACTIVE HOME MEETINGS— WHICH IS MORE SCRIPTURAL?

For the first 300 years of church history, churches met in homes. The first church buildings didn't arrive on the scene until the days of Constantine. We're told little about what meetings of the church looked like in the first century, with the exception of a passage in I Corinthians chapter 14. There we read, "*What is the outcome then, brethren? When you assemble, each one has a psalm, has a teaching, has a revelation, has a tongue, has an interpretation. Let all things be done for edification" (I Cor. 14:26).*

I'd like you to ask yourself, do you ever get tired of going to church Sunday after Sunday and getting preached to all the time? Granted, there are some gifted speakers that can minister Christ (and many that cannot), but if you were honest with yourself, wouldn't you admit that you get pretty tired of going to a place 52 weeks a year and listening to the same person preach? Many Christians today have the ingrained mentality that going to a church meeting means going to the same place every Sunday morning to hear one person—the same person—pontificate. Where do the Scriptures teach that?

We do find situations in the New Testament where people gathered to hear gifted leaders teach, but these were not the kinds of meetings I Corinthians 14 describes when it addresses the issue of what believers are to do when they assemble together.

In Acts 2:42, Luke records that the apostles taught the masses in the temple. This, however, was a short-lived situation lasting only a few years because those meetings ceased abruptly when persecution came to the church in Jerusalem. While the apostles were free to teach publicly, and people did go to the temple to receive instruction, the church in Jerusalem continued to meet in homes all during this time, *"breaking bread from house to house, they were taking their meals together with gladness and sincerity of heart, praising God and having favor with all the people..."* (Acts 2:46-47).

So those temple meetings can't be used as a scriptural precedent to prop up the current way the great majority of Christians practice "church" today, by going to a designated place each week to hear a person preach.

Paul also taught for two years at the School of Tyrannus in Ephesus where he held "discipleship classes" for future church planters. But those meetings were separate from the I Corinthian 14 type of church meetings that continued to be held in various locations throughout the city in people's homes.

In Acts 28:30-31 we also see another example of Paul teaching *"all who came to him"* in a rented space while under house arrest in Rome. But those special teaching meetings were also something additional that people could attend outside of the normal I Corinthian 14 type of church meetings that were taking place in various locations around Rome in people's homes.

Are you weary of having your main responsibility as a Christian reduced to coming to a large gathering Sunday after Sunday and sitting passively on your hands as you watch a Christian performance conducted by a select few "professionals" that dominate the whole meeting? I have some good news for you. While the Scriptures do not prohibit any one type of church meeting, I Corinthians 14:26-40 gives us a scriptural precedent showing what a Christian meeting in New Testament times actually looked like. That passage contains statements like,

> *What is the outcome then, brethren (brothers and sisters)? When you assemble, **each one** has a psalm, has a teaching, has a revelation, has a tongue, has an interpretation. Let all things be done for edification.*
>
> [I Cor. 14:26, Emphasis mine]

> *Let **two** or **three prophets speak**, and let the others pass judgment. But if a revelation is made to another who is seated, the first one must keep silent. For **you can all prophesy one by one**, so that all may learn and all may be exhorted; and the spirit of the prophets are subject to prophets; for God is not a God of confusion but of peace, as in all the churches of the saints.*
>
> [Emphasis mine]

Here we see that the environment in meetings of the early church was such that *each one* could participate, and *all* could prophesy. When was the last time you saw that in a Sunday morning church service?

Take a moment and try to imagine that happening. Imagine that you are in a traditional Sunday morning church service somewhere, and while the pastor is preaching a sermon, the Lord speaks something to you. Now envision yourself standing up and motioning to the pastor to sit down as you turn to the congregation and begin sharing what God has revealed to you. What do you see next? You probably see yourself swarmed upon by a few large bodies and being quickly ushered out of the building!

To press the point even further, let's say that when the pastor finishes his sermon, you feel like the Lord had given you something to say that would adjust or balance his message. Something he said was not quite right according to the Scriptures or left people with the wrong impression. You stand up and say, "Pastor so and so, that was a good message, but I think some would disagree with you when you said…, and it might have left the wrong impression. I'd like to clear that up by saying…." Try that even once or twice, and you'll likely be branded as contentious and rebellious and be blackballed from that and possibly every other Christian meeting in the vicinity. That's no exaggeration.

Yet this Scripture shows us that meeting in an informal environment, where *each one* was free to contribute, was standard fare when it came to first-century style church meetings. Can you see what a safeguard this is for God's people? Wouldn't such an environment cause a minister to think twice about taking advantage of a captive audience, knowing that his words would be tested and judged? Today's monologue sermons put pastors and preachers in the same power-position as a dentist who has you in his chair and has all his instruments and gadgets in your

> *Today's monologue sermons put pastors and preachers in the same power-position as a dentist who has you in his chair and has all his instruments and gadgets in your mouth while he works on your teeth. All the while he is free to lecture you about anything he wants, but you have no way to respond.*

mouth while he works on your teeth. All the while he is free to lecture you about anything he wants, but you have no way to respond.

"SITTERS' RIGHTS"

Throughout this book I have addressed the idea of recovery or rebuilding God's house based on its original design. By this I mean reinstating things that have been lost over the years to their rightful place within the church.

The Reformation of the 1500s brought about the great divide between Protestants and Catholics, resulting in the formation of the state church. Many who were initially on the side of Calvin, Luther, and Zwingli however, felt that the changes these Reformation leaders brought about did not go far enough. But with political power now on their side, the reformers intolerantly attempted to quash any voice of dissent that questioned their authority and that of the state church.

The people on whom these reformers came down the hardest became known as the Anabaptists, that is, the re-baptizers. They got their name because they believed that baptism should only be for those who had truly repented and found new life in Christ, while the state church believed in infant baptism.

The Anabaptists believed in returning to the simplicity of the church as found in the New Testament. Most of the Anabaptists were young people. They preached on street corners, baptized new believers, and celebrated the Lord's Supper in homes.

In his excellent book about the Anabaptists, Peter Hoover writes,

This was sedition! This was high treason! "Unauthorized men preaching on the street corners" wrote Martin Luther "are a sure sign of the devil." John, duke of Saxony, made a law at once to stop secret baptisms and communions. Imagine! Baptizing or celebrating communion without the church's consent! Without buildings but in private homes! This, wrote Luther, is blasphemy, blasphemy, blasphemy…and after his book *Of the Sneaky Ones and the Corner Preachers* came book after book and sermon after sermon loaded with his bitterest invectives against the Anabaptists who "dared to take the Scriptures into their own hands and overthrow the authority of the church."

As a result, being an Anabaptist became a capital offense. They were severely persecuted and hundreds of thousands were drowned, burned at the stake, and beheaded—all in the name of Christ.

Regarding their practice of meeting together, these Anabaptists held to a teaching they called "Sitzrecht," which in English is translated "sitters' right." Peter Hoover continues,

> The Anabaptists took literally the words of Paul in I Corinthians 14:30-31: "And if a revelation comes to someone who is sitting down, the first speaker should stop. For you can all prophesy in turn so that everyone may be instructed and encouraged." They called this the "sitters' right" and calmly implied that they, when moved by inner conviction, had as great a right to speak and to act as any pastor, any priest, any reformer or bishop or pope. The audacity, this "Sitzrecht from the pit of hell," Martin Luther and his friends believed, could be dealt with only by fire, water, and the sword"

Five hundred years ago if there were those, as there are in our day, advocating participatory, interactive church meetings, they would have been numbered among the Anabaptists and probably been burnt at the stake or drowned. Unthinkable as that may seem, many of your friends and mine would probably now be dead and I wouldn't have lived long enough to write this book! Thank God we live in a different country and a different era.

The value of something is what someone is willing to pay for it. I bring up the point of the Anabaptists to show that people and groups throughout the centuries have spoken and acted in favor of returning to the kind of meetings that Paul wrote about in I Corinthians chapter 14—even being willing to pay the ultimate price in order to do so.

God intends for the church to be a place where each believer can

Five hundred years ago if there were those, as there are in our day, advocating participatory, interactive church meetings, they would have been numbered among the Anabaptists and probably been burnt at the stake or drowned. Unthinkable as that may seem, many of your friends and mine would probably now be dead.

freely employ every gift God has given him or her for mutual edification and for building up the body of Christ as a whole. But that can only happen in the proper environment. In the early church there was no clergy-laity system, no Christian caste system. But over time, the ways of the world crept into the church and eventually took up permanent residence.

As a result, the norm in churches today is that the power, the functioning, and the authority are in the hands of the high-caste tier—the clergy—relegating the common "layman" to second-class status, thus marginalizing their participation, importance, ingenuity, creativity, and growth.

Any group of Christians intent on seeing the recovery and restoration of the church and advancing beyond chapter five of Nehemiah, will require a radical reassessment of their understanding of spiritual authority, and the elimination of the clergy-laity system.

You may be asking yourself why dismantling the clergy-laity system is so important that I am spending so much time making the point. Just as it is extremely important how the components, parts, and systems of the human body relate to each other, the same holds true with how leaders relate with other members in the body of Christ. At an even more basic level, this relationship raises the issue, how is the kingdom of God governed?

THE ORIGINS OF THIS WORLD'S SYSTEM

To understand how the kingdom of God is governed, we need to go all the way back to the Garden of Eden. There we see the origin of an alien kingdom and the world system that was set up in opposition to the kingdom of God.

We live in a fallen world. God's original purpose for mankind was that they bear the image of God and rule the earth, which included ruling over the creeping things (Gen. 1:26-28). Satan, however, came to the man and the woman in the garden in the form of a snake and deceived them. Instead of ruling over and subduing the creeping things, the enemy got the upper hand and began building his kingdom on this earth through fallen man.

In Genesis chapter four we read that Cain went out from the presence of God and built the first city. Cities became the habitat of fallen man and places where men and women sought to find security and significance outside of the presence of God.

Within these cities men developed governments, formed militaries, and established educational systems. Hierarchical systems of leadership and authority began to emerge to maintain order and control.

We see how this world system has developed and been magnified in our day. Look at our military: generals, colonels, majors, lieutenants, sergeants, and at the bottom, the garden-variety, enlisted men. Look at the postal system, the judicial system, our educational system, and the management structure in any corporation. Where did this hierarchical, chain-of-command type of system originate?

Going back to the days of King Darius (who ruled between the time of Nebuchadnezzar and Cyrus), we can discover what form of rule and government he set in place over his kingdom. He appointed satraps, or vassal kings, to be protectors of his kingdom, and over them commissioners. It is the same chain-of-command system that we see all around us today:

> *It seemed good to Darius to appoint 120 satraps over the kingdom, that they would be in charge of the whole kingdom, and over them three commissioners (of whom Daniel was one), that these satraps might be accountable to them, and that the king might not suffer loss.*
>
> (Dan. 6:1, 2)

The remnant that returned from Babylon to Jerusalem to rebuild the temple lived under this type of system. As time marched on, the Greeks became the next great empire, followed by the Romans, who ruled during and long after the time of the New Testament.

By the third century A.D., Constantine made Christianity the official religion of the Roman Empire. The church and the state were wed. The church became more and more institutionalized and influenced by the world. Interestingly, a similar structure, seen in Rome's political system, found its way into the Catholic Church. A hierarchical church "government" crystallized, with the pope at the top, and beneath him 70 cardinals, and beneath them archbishops, bishops, priests, and finally, at the bottom rung of this hierarchical system, the masses of common lay people.

This hierarchical, chain-of-command system of rule and authority can easily be traced back to the Persian and Babylonian Empires, and more likely, back to the original city of Babel, the first city organized by fallen man at the dawn of civilization. But did it have an even earlier origin than that?

The Bible teaches that all authority comes from God. The question is: Does God want a hierarchical system of authority in his church? Is this the way the kingdom of God is governed? Is this the way God governs his own house?

> *The Bible teaches that all authority comes from God. The question is: Does God want a hierarchical system of authority in his church?*

Clearly, we can find in the Scriptures one species in God's creation that operates under this hierarchical type of system. It's the angels. God ordained archangels (including Michael, Gabriel, and Lucifer, the fallen archangel) and under these archangels are the angels, demons, and principalities. So, this hierarchical system was ordained by God—at least for angels. But did God ever intend this system for the sons and daughters of God?

How Is the Kingdom of God Governed?

Searching the Old Testament for some examples, we see that Moses' father-in-law Jethro, a Bedouin nomad, influenced him to select leaders to place over the people—a hierarchy of leaders, some over thousands of people, some over hundreds, some over fifties, and some over tens (Exod. chapter 18). This seemed to Moses to be a good idea at the time, but we're not told that this idea of Jethro's was inspired by God.

By comparison, later in the book of Numbers, we see God taking the initiative in appointing delegated authority when he said to Moses:

> *"Gather for Me seventy men from the elders of Israel, whom you know to be the elders of the people and their officers and bring them to the tent of meeting, and let them take their stand there with you. Then I will come down and speak with you there, and I will take of the Spirit who is upon you, and will put Him upon them; and they shall bear the burden of the people with you, so that you shall not bear it all alone."*
>
> (Num. 11:16-17)

This time, when God spoke to Moses about delegated authority, it was spiritual in nature, and there was no mention of a chain-of-command.

Another interesting observation relating to the kind of rule God intends for his kingdom comes from the story in I Samuel where the people of Israel wanted Samuel to choose a king to rule over them. They wanted to be like "all the nations," with a king who would judge for them and go out before them to fight their battles.

God warned them through Samuel:

> *So Samuel spoke all the words of the Lord to the people who had asked of him a king. He said, "This will be the procedure of the king who will reign over you: he will take your sons and place them for himself in his chariots and among his horsemen and they will run before his chariots.* **He will appoint for himself commanders of thousands and of fifties,** *and some to do his plowing and to reap his harvest and to make his weapons of war and equipment for his chariots. He will take your daughters for perfumers and cooks and bakers. He will take the best of your*

fields and your vineyards and your olive groves and give them to his servants. He will take a tenth of your seed and of your vineyards and give to his officers and to his servants. He will also take your male servants and your female servants and your best young men and your donkeys and use them for his work. He will take a tenth of your flocks, and you yourselves will become his servants. Then you will cry out in that day because of your king whom you have chosen for yourselves, but the Lord will not answer you in that day."

(I Sam. 8:10-18) [Emphasis mine]

The people did a foolish thing by asking for a king. Samuel was displeased with their request, and he sought the Lord about it. God's response was: *"Listen to the voice of the people in regard to all that they say to you, for they have not rejected you, but they have rejected Me from being king over them" (I Sam. 8:7).* Even so, God gave them a king, though in the passage above we see that he told the people what would happen under this king. Included in this description is a hierarchical structure of government.

IN GOD'S KINGDOM, GOD IS KING!

The people asked for a king, but in a sense, they already had one—they were already in a kingdom. In God's kingdom, God is King! In God's kingdom people have direct access to their king. Rather strange, in comparison with earthly kingdoms! In the kingdom of God, direct access to authority is not several people removed.

> *In God's kingdom people have direct access to their king. Rather strange, in comparison with earthly kingdoms! In the kingdom of God, direct access to authority is not several people removed.*

God intended this hierarchical, chain-of-command system to maintain rule, order, and authority for angels—not for the sons and daughters of God! This system was introduced to our planet by Satan, a fallen archangel, intent on building his own kingdom on the earth through fallen man. Sadly, this system has made inroads into the church. The last thing that Satan wants to see is men and women leaving his kingdom, returning to the place of living in the presence of God, both individually and corporately, and having direct access to God alone as their King.

In Ephesians chapter one we're told that Christ was raised from the dead and is seated at God's right hand, *"far above all rule and authority and power and dominion, and every name that is named, not only in this age, but also in the one to come."* Later, in chapter two, it says that God *"raised us up with Him, and seated us with Him in the heavenly places, in Christ Jesus."* Not only is Christ far above all rule and authority (including that hierarchical form ordained for angels), but so are we! So is his church. We are in him!

If this sounds like a dangerous teaching, analogous to giving a child a hand grenade to play with in the street, wait just a minute. I am not advocating total anarchy and the throwing off of all rule and subjection to anyone except God. Let me explain.

Spiritual Authority in the Church: Who Are the Greatest and Who Are the Leaders

During Jesus' life on earth, the twelve disciples had some idea that he had come to establish a new kingdom. But what kind of kingdom? The twelve were subjects of the Roman Empire, so they understood a hierarchical form of government. In Matthew chapter 20, the question arose concerning who would sit at his right hand and who would sit at his left. The implied question lurking in their hearts was, "Lord, in your kingdom you will be King, but as number two or number three in charge, who am I going to get to rule over?"

Carnal man wants power, control, and authority over others. Look at the other religions of the world, religions that are not of God. In Hinduism, the sacred writings are written in Sanskrit, which the common people can't read or understand. So the Hindus need special priests to interpret the teachings of Hinduism for them. In Islam, Imams are in control. They're the ones who interpret the Koran for the other Muslims who do not have or cannot read the holy writings that tell them how to live their lives. Judaism has its rabbis, which act as intermediaries to interpret the laws for people. And for centuries, Catholic priests gave the mass in Latin, which virtually no one understood, thus securing for themselves an elevated place of power and erecting themselves as the true custodians of the knowledge of God and the teachings of the church.

If you trace it all the way back to the beginning, Satan was the one that appeared to the man and woman in the garden and presented himself to them as an intermediary. Though a false messenger, the man and the woman succumbed to listening to someone else interpret God's will for them rather than relying on God himself. In all of the religions you have men (or women) who want to be in the power position of interpreting the will of God for others and having others subject to them. In Hinduism it's the priests, in Buddhism, it's the monks, in Islam it's the Imams, in Judaism it's the rabbis, in Catholicism it's the priests, and in Protestantism it's the...

In the story from Matthew chapter 20 and Luke chapter 22 about Jesus' disciples, Jesus knew the carnal mindset of his followers, which was no different than the mindset of other fallen men and women in any other culture of the world. He gave them some very pointed and very surprising instructions about who would be the greatest, and what those leaders would look like in the kingdom of God:

> *"The kings of the Gentiles lord it over them; and those who have authority over them are called 'Benefactors.' But it is not this way with you, but the one who is the greatest among you must become like the youngest, and the leader as the servant."*
>
> (Luke 22:25-26)

In this passage, the disciples got something they probably never expected. This question of spiritual authority in the church can be somewhat confusing. How can the "greatest" in the church be as the youngest (children), and how can the leaders be as servants (slaves)? Ironically, it's the children and slaves in society who have the least authority of all. You could even say that they are the ones with *no* authority!

> *How can the "greatest" in the church be as the youngest (children), and how can the leaders be as servants (slaves)? Ironically, it's the children and slaves in society who have the least authority of all. You could even say that they are the ones with no authority!*

In a hierarchical, chain-of-command system, those in higher positions have authority over those under them. Authority comes with position, and with position comes title. For example, if you were a private or enlisted person in the military, and a four-star general approached you and ordered you to pick up a cigarette butt on the ground, you would salute him, say, "Yes, sir!" and immediately carry out the order. And if you didn't, you'd be sorry and probably never make that mistake again!

But let's say that general retires from the military, and one day you're walking along the road and see him in his civilian clothes. He recognizes you and the two of you stop to have a brief conversation. During that conversation he looks down, sees a cigarette butt, and orders you to pick it up. *Now* you have some options. He's no longer in the military, so you could *choose* to follow that order if you wanted to, but you are no longer under obligation to do it. On the other hand, if you wanted to, you could in no uncertain terms tell him to pick it up himself!

In the hierarchical system you pay respect to those with titles who are in authority over you and you follow their orders. Importantly, the authority is linked with the position or title, not necessarily with one's character.

In his letters to Timothy, Paul spilled a good deal of ink describing leaders and setting out qualifications for elders and deacons—positions of responsibility in the church. But notice his emphasis on character and on being servant leaders. In the church, leadership is based on character, on the manifestation of the Spirit's fruits in one's life, and on being a good role model in serving others.

But can we find anywhere in the Bible where our church leaders are given direct "authority over" those in the flock? It makes for an interesting study to see who has been given authority by God, and specifically, who has been given authority over whom.

The New Testament clearly teaches that God has authority, Christ has authority, the Spirit has authority, angels have authority, demons have authority, principalities and powers have authority, and some humans have authority. Kings have been given authority by God (Rom. 13:1-2); the disciples were given authority over unclean spirits (Matt. 10:1); believers have the authority to become children of God (John 1:12); but nowhere does it explicitly say that one believer has authority over another believer!

Can one believer speak the word of God to another believer? Most certainly! In speaking the word from God are we not acting as ambassadors of Christ, and shouldn't that word be heeded? Absolutely. But it bears repeating that nowhere do the Scriptures say that one believer has authority over another believer!

Here in America we saw great abuses of authority in what was called the "Shepherding Movement," that began in the 1970s. Many well-meaning evangelical and charismatic leaders put a system in place whereby every Christian had to have someone "over" him or her. Each Christian needed a "spiritual covering." What resulted were terrible abuses of power. Christians were telling other Christians whom they should marry, what jobs they should take, and how to order the affairs of their families. It even went so far as Christians being told that they should divorce their Christian spouses if the spouses were not going along with the church and with the church's leadership structure. Fortunately, many people involved in this movement saw the error of it and got out. But it was not without a terrible cost to countless numbers of believers.

DON'T THE SCRIPTURES SAY TO "OBEY YOUR LEADERS?"

I sympathize with Christians all over the world who want to obey the Lord and do what the Bible says. But sometimes poor translations from the original texts keep us from gaining a crystal clear understanding of the intended meaning of certain Scriptures. Take the verse in Hebrews 13:17 as a good example: *"Obey your leaders and submit to them, for they keep watch over your souls as those who will give an account."*

The word translated "obey" is not the primary word in the original language used to mean "obey," but more accurately means, "let yourself be persuaded by." The word used for "submit" is not an order, but rather it means "to yield" or "to give in." So this verse actually says (my paraphrase): Allow yourselves to be persuaded by your leaders (because of their example, their godly character, their servant natures, and their familiarity with God's ways and his truth) and be willing to yield to them.

Both words for "obey" and "submit" communicate the notion that there is a choice involved. People are not being admonished to mindlessly obey out of fear, as a soldier would with an order given by a military commander. This is not the relationship God intended to exist between church leaders and other members of the body of Christ.

As Christians, we are to be in total obedience and submission to God. To other men, however, we are to give total submission but limited obedience. Submission is an attitude. Obedience is an action. The apostles had an attitude of submission to the authorities in Jerusalem, but they could not obey when told to stop speaking the things of the Lord.

> *As Christians, we are to be in total obedience and submission to God. To other men, however, we are to give total submission but limited obedience. Submission is an attitude. Obedience is an action.*

Jesus had an attitude of submission to Pontius Pilate, but total obedience was reserved for his Father alone. When there is a conflict in submitting to authorities (or to one another), we should always try to maintain an attitude of submission (as opposed to rebellion), yet obey the higher authority.

LEADERS IN THE CHURCH NEED TO BE GOOD "PERSUADERS"

Francis of Assisi once said, "Preach the gospel at all times, and when necessary use words." This idea is consistent with the apostle Paul's criterion for leadership in the church. It's not primarily based on how well a person can preach or teach, but on character (see Paul's qualifications for elders and deacons in I Tim. 3:1-15).

We should want to imitate our leaders because of the way they live their lives and as a result, allow ourselves to be influenced by what they say. We're not called to mindlessly obey those in Christian leadership who may hold prominent titles, positions (in some sort of appointed hierarchy), or possess a natural gift for oratory but who are deficient as far as earning our respect because of their spiritual character. Let me illustrate with another example:

Recently I visited a Christian group in Russia. I overheard a conversation that a leader there was having with one of the other church members. This leader wanted very much to launch a prison ministry and for this brother whom he was speaking with to head it up. But this brother had no desire whatsoever to do that. He had been in prison and it had been a terrible experience—one that he didn't want to be reminded of. His heart was not willing or ready to take on the responsibility for a prison ministry. Yet his "pastor" kept insisting.

I didn't stick around long enough to see if or how the situation was resolved. But I do know that the pastor was using guilt, manipulation, and his "position" to try to get that brother to do what he did not want to do. He probably felt justified because he was the "pastor" and that brother was supposed to "obey" his leader. The poor brother, on the other hand, even if he prevailed and was able to convince the pastor that someone else should do the job, most likely walked away feeling guilty. He probably felt that he was a bad "Christian" because he did not obey or submit to the Christian leader that was "over him."

It's dreadful to think how often situations like this are repeated in Christendom throughout the world. A faulty understanding of spiritual authority, who should have it, and how to use it, has two adverse effects in the church. First, it fuels pride and helps perpetuate the abominable clergy-laity system that we are told in Revelation, the Lord hates. John wrote to the Ephesian church that they hated the deeds of the Nicolaitans, which the Lord also hated (Rev. 2:6). *Nico* means "rule over." *Laos* means "the common people." All the way back in the first century this disease of an elite class of professional Christians ruling over the common folk was attempting to take root in the churches. In one of his epistles, the apostle John dealt directly with such a person:

> *I wrote something to the church; but Diotrephes, who loves to be first among them, does not accept what we say. For this reason, if I come, I will call attention to his deeds which he does, unjustly accusing us with wicked words; and not satisfied with this, he himself does not receive the brethren, either, and he forbids those who desire to do so and puts them out of the church. Beloved, do not imitate what is evil, but what is good. The one who does good is of God; but the one who does evil has not seen God.*
> (III John: 1, 9-11)

The second problem created by a faulty understanding of spiritual authority is that those on the receiving end of commands and admonitions by Christian leaders who wield their "authority" are often wounded with a sense of unwarranted guilt for not being able to obey their leaders. They feel like they have failed as Christians when in reality, they may not have had the maturity (or received the instruction) to know of their freedom in Christ. They may not have been taught that Christ dwells within them and wants to be their Lord and that they are only called to unconditionally obey the Lord alone.

PAUL, THE SPIRITUAL FATHER AND LOVING PERSUADER

Paul's letter to Philemon gives us a wonderful insight into a man who had been given authority by God to build up the church. In this brief letter we see the heart of a father, expressed in loving persuasion to one of Paul's spiritual sons in the Lord, Philemon.

Philemon was a wealthy businessman from the town of Colosse (about 100 miles east of Ephesus). He owned a slave by the name of Onesimus. On Paul's third missionary journey, probably while in Ephesus, he met Philemon and led him to Christ. From that time Philemon became a help to Paul. Some five years later from a prison in Rome, Paul wrote to Philemon. His letter concerned the runaway slave, Onesimus. Onesimus had run away from his master and found Paul in Rome. Paul then led Onesimus to the Lord.

Savor Paul's words as he addressed Philemon, his own child in the faith, and pled with him to do the right thing in regard to Onesimus:

> *Paul's letter to Philemon gives us a wonderful insight into a man who had been given authority by God to build up the church. In this brief letter we see the heart of a father, expressed in loving persuasion to one of Paul's spiritual sons in the Lord, Philemon.*

I thank my God always, making mention of you in my prayers, because I hear of your love, and of the faith which you have toward the Lord Jesus, and toward all the saints; and I pray that the fellowship of your faith may become effective through the knowledge of every good thing which is in you for Christ's sake. For I have come to have much joy and comfort in your love, because the hearts of the saints have been refreshed through you, brother. Therefore, though I have much confidence in Christ to order you to do that which is proper, yet for love's sake I rather appeal to you—since I am such a person as Paul, the aged, and now also a prisoner of Christ Jesus—I appeal to you for my child, whom I have begotten in my imprisonment, Onesimus, who formerly was useless to you, but now is useful both to you and to me. And I have sent him back to you in person, that is, sending my very heart, whom I wished to keep with me, that in your behalf he might minister to me in my imprisonment for the gospel; but without your consent I did not want to do anything, that your goodness should not be as it were by compulsion, but of your own free will.

(Phil. 4-14)

Do you get the sense here that Paul was one who was anxious to exercise his spiritual authority? After all, Philemon owed Paul his life, for Paul led him to Christ. Rather than ordering Philemon what to do in regard to Onesimus, Paul reasoned with him. He persuaded him. He lovingly built a case, giving Philemon a choice to do what was right. This shows that Paul was a man who truly knew what spiritual authority was and how it was to be used.

The Christian message is such a radical one! In the kingdom of God, God is king. He wants each of his children to have access to him directly. Christianity is not like the religions in the world system—including fallen Christianity—with layers of intermediaries between the common man and God. Jesus came to live and to die, to rise again, and to become the life-giving Spirit so that he could indwell all those who believe, so that we all can know him directly and personally, from the least to the greatest.

On a personal note, I want to share two stories that relate to this matter of spiritual authority. The first, concerning the man who was my "spiritual father."

Years ago God placed a man in my life who laid the foundation for my knowing Christ. I have not seen or spent much time with him in the past 25 years, but I still consider him to have been a spiritual father to me. But is he my spiritual authority? Is he still my "spiritual covering" in the Lord? Of course not! If I were to see him today and to seek his advice or counsel, I would give serious consideration to what he said in response because I respect his knowledge and understanding of the Lord. But we have a different relationship now than we did 30 years ago. He taught me to know Christ, and I still respect him and appreciate him, but our relationship is now that of being brothers in the Lord.

I also think of my relationship with my two daughters. One is in her thirties and married, the mother of two. The other is in her twenties and is also married. Both are Christians and are following the Lord. I am so proud of both of them.

Though they are married, I am still their father. So, do I have "spiritual authority" over them? No. My wife and I have done our best to encourage our daughters to know Christ and to learn to follow him for themselves. We don't expect "mindless obedience" from them. Rather, our role is to encourage them, to be in their corner believing in them, to tell them how much we love them, to pray for them, and to try to be their greatest fans.

When they come to confide in us or seek advice, we give it to them. But they are now at the age when the choice to follow that advice is theirs. If we want to be an influence, we need to maintain their respect by the way we live our lives, and get better and better at becoming "loving persuaders," just like the apostle Paul.

With all these things in mind, if you are in a position of leadership, I have these words of advice for you:

1. Put little stock in having a title—whether it be pastor, reverend, bishop, or anything else. As a matter of fact, I advise you to refuse to be called by any elevating title. Instead, why not just let yourself be called by the title that puts all of the Lord's followers on the same high and lofty level, which our Lord himself advocated for us to take: brother or sister? (see Matt. 23:8-12)
2. Be like loving fathers to those you work with.
3. Don't expect mindless obedience, or you'll set yourself up for disappointment because you don't really comprehend how to use the "authority" God has given you to build others up. Your goal should be to bring others to the point of knowing Christ's authority in their own lives for themselves.
4. Teach people to live under the authority of Christ.
5. Expect that one day those for whom you are caring and acting as a guide will leave you.
6. Hope that one day those who leave you will come back to you, and that you will have a relationship with them as a brother or sister, and as a friend.

Having come to this point in understanding spiritual authority, our challenge is in applying what we have learned. How do we relate to our brothers and sisters in Christ, understanding and recognizing God's delegated authority in others but not giving in to the hierarchical rules of submission and authority that were intended for a lower species of life-forms—the angels—rather than for the sons and daughters of God? By God's grace we can handle the challenge, and as individuals or corporate groups of people, we can move further down the road that leads to recovery and rebuilding of God's house as it was always intended to be.

Chapter Ten

HEARING THE WORD OF GOD AND ABIDING IN CHRIST
EZRA'S REAPPEARANCE IN THE BOOK OF NEHEMIAH

So the wall was completed on the twenty-fifth day of Elul, in fifty-two days. When all our enemies heard of it, and all the nations surrounding us saw it, they lost their confidence; for they recognized that this work had been accomplished with the help of our God.

(Neh. 6:15, 16)

The work to complete the wall was laborious, time-consuming, and fraught with danger. But with the wall completed, the unity was restored. God's enemies on the outside lost their confidence. Nehemiah chapter seven tells us the doors of the gates were hung, and the gatekeepers, singers, and Levites were appointed.

Who were the gatekeepers? A walled city with no gates would have been a prison. Jerusalem had to have gates, and they needed gatekeepers. The gatekeepers performed the important tasks of keeping inside what should stay inside, keeping outside what should stay outside, and allowing appropriate transit between the two.

Spiritually, these gatekeepers represent elders or the spiritual leaders that God raises up within his body. They are the ones that "keep the bad guys out." If you've been a part of any group of Christians for a significant time, you instinctively know who these people are. They don't need to advertise that position by having a title hung around their necks. God's people know who to turn to in times of trouble or crisis. They know who has been given spiritual oversight and who has been gifted to lead.

In addition to the gatekeepers, there were also the singers and Levites—those who worship and those who serve.

Nehemiah 7:3 says, *"Do not let the gates of Jerusalem be opened until the sun is hot."* This tells us that the life in God's city, behind the protective wall, was to be a life conducted completely in the light. We as the Lord's people today must live together in the light if we are to experience true fellowship in Christ. In the words of the apostle John,

> *This is the message we have heard from Him and announce to you, that God is Light, and in Him there is no darkness at all. If we say that we have fellowship with Him and yet walk in the darkness, we lie and do not practice the truth; but if we walk in the Light as He Himself is in the Light, we have fellowship with one another, and the blood of Jesus His Son cleanses us from all sin.*
>
> (I John 1:5-7)

FURTHER SIGNIFICANCE OF THE WALL

With the wall built and the enemies from within and without under control, the people were free to become a strong and cohesive unit. Proper relationships had been restored. The problems between the leaders and the people had been resolved. There was unity. Through all the building, serving, standing with one another, fighting together, and by each one stepping up to reclaim his rightful place and responsibility, the physical wall around Jerusalem was completed.

This physical wall not only meant protection and separation from the world, but it also represented the strength and unity that had been built between the people.

Have you ever seen a stone wall? When you look at it, what do you see? You see many stones tightly packed together into one unit. When the psalmist David wrote about Jerusalem he said, *"I was glad when they said to me, 'Let us go to the house of the Lord.' Our feet are standing within your gates, O Jerusalem, Jerusalem, that is built as a city that is compact together…" (Ps. 122:1-3).*

> *Have you ever seen a stone wall? When you look at it, what do you see? You see many stones tightly packed together into one unit.*

The Oxford Annotated Bible translates Psalm 122:3, *"Jerusalem—built as a city that is bound firmly together,"* while the 21st Century King James Version states it this way: *"Jerusalem is a built as a city that is united together."*

We are God's living stones. He wants to build us up together with other saints by the transforming power of his life into a protective wall that displays to the world our unity in Christ.

This Old Testament picture shows us that with the wall completed, Jerusalem had peace, protection, and unity. In fact, unity can itself be a wall of protection for God's people. The greatest example of this is in the book of Revelation, where John saw the heavenly city, New Jerusalem coming down from heaven to the new earth. John saw the wall of that city, and described it in Rev. 21:12-14. Verse 14 says, *"and the wall of the city had twelve foundation stones, and on them were the twelve names of the twelve apostles of the Lamb."*

The heavenly city, New Jerusalem, is built upon the foundation of the apostles. For three-and-a-half years, our Lord built them together as a unit. They were transformed by his grace. By living constantly with him and with one another, they were changed. By the time the day of Pentecost had come, there was never a group of people so built together as one and so prepared to actually be the foundation of church. Their knowledge of Christ and the unity this produced was the foundation upon which the entire church was built. This unity was a wall of protection for the church from the enemies that would come against it.

An example of this is seen when the rulers, elders and scribes, including Annas the high priest, and Caiaphas arrested Peter and John and commanded them to speak no longer to any man in Jesus' name. The two apostles together replied, *"Whether it is right in the sight of God to give heed to you rather than to God, you be the judge; for we cannot stop speaking about what we have seen and heard" (Acts 4:19, 20).* Upon seeing and hearing their unified response, the rulers could do nothing more than to threaten them and let them go.

A THIRD REVIVAL

So far we've seen two revivals in the story of Ezra. The first was when the people came back from Babylon, the land of confusion, to Jerusalem, the city of peace. They came with laughing and shouts of joy. Being delivered from the land of confusion and false religion to the place where the house of God is built on the original foundation brought revival and great joy to the Lord's people.

Next, we saw the second revival when the people were down and discouraged but responded to the message of the prophets Haggai and Zechariah. These prophets pointed the people to look for Christ, the Desire of All Nations who was to come, and they rose up, were revived, and finished the work on the temple.

Now we come to a third revival. The people needed to come to life once more. This third revival occurred when they began to understand the word of God for themselves.

In Nehemiah 8:1, Ezra, who had returned to Jerusalem with his heart intent on teaching the word of God, now returns on the scene. The remnant was now gathered together once again as one man at the square in front of the Water Gate to hear the Law read and interpreted. Spiritually, gathering in front of the Water Gate speaks of their thirst for the living water that comes from the word of God. This event took place on the first day of the seventh month, reminding them (and us) that in order to receive the living water, they (and we) need to be resting in God.

In Nehemiah 8:9 we read, *"For all the people were weeping when they heard the words of the law."* Why were they weeping when they heard the Law read? Was it because they were convicted of sin? Or was it because they had begun to understand the demands of a righteous God and knew that in themselves, they could not meet them?

When Nehemiah saw the people weeping, he said to them, *"Go, eat of the fat, drink of the sweet, and send portions to him who has nothing prepared; for this day is holy to our Lord. Do not be grieved, for the joy of the Lord is your strength" (Neh. 8:10).* Their strength to perform the Law was not in themselves. They needed to see that the joy of the Lord was their strength. (The joy of the Lord is Christ!)

The following day they gathered again and received more insight. *"They found written in the law how the Lord had commanded through Moses that the sons of Israel should live in booths during the feast of the seventh month" (Neh. 8:14).* Having heard what God commanded Israel to do, the people responded. They went out and got leafy branches and made temporary shelters, or booths, and lived in them for seven days. Verse 17 says that there was "great rejoicing." Revival had come once again to the people for the third time.

Why did they rejoice? Spiritually speaking, they learned that the joy of the Lord was their strength and that they could obey the words of the Law only by abiding in Christ, represented by abiding or living in the booths. For a full week these booths became the people's homes where they lived, ate, slept, prayed, meditated, and rested. The Feast of Booths was a physical illustration for what Luke wrote in the New Testament, *"For in him we live, and move, and have our being…" (Acts 17:28a KJV).*

The same people that had responded with tears when they heard the Law read, now in Christ, found joy and strength.

> *The same people that had responded with tears when they heard the Law read, now in Christ, found joy and strength.*

A BETTER OATH

Following their celebration by living in the booths, the people were once again convicted of their sins: *"The descendants of Israel separated themselves from all foreigners, and stood and confessed their sins and the iniquities of their fathers" (Neh. 9:2).* This led them to make another vow to the Lord (Neh. 9:38 and Neh. chapter ten). This time they put it in writing. They vowed to walk in God's law and to keep and observe all the commandments of their God (including not giving their sons or daughters to marry the heathen of the land). Though similar to the first oath recorded in the book of Ezra, which they failed to keep, this oath was different.

In the first oath the people vowed to quit sinning and to put away their foreign wives. But that didn't work. This was an "Old Covenant" vow—try harder. Just "do it."

In this new vow however, we see three characteristics that were different. The first was a dedication to walk in the law of God and to keep all the commandments of God. Spiritually speaking, this was a dedication to listen and respond to the word of God. This is something that we as Christians can and should do. We can give ourselves to the Lord, and dedicate ourselves to hearing and responding to his word.

In this new vow the people also said that they would honor the Sabbath. Spiritually speaking, they understood that they could only please God and keep his law by honoring the Sabbath, which in new covenant terms, represents resting in Christ.

Third, they dedicated themselves to tithing—to bringing in the first fruits, the first of their herds and their flocks, the first of their dough, and their new wine. They also dedicated their firstborn sons to the Lord.

Spiritually, this represents surrender. We know that everything belongs to God. He does not need our tithe. But tithing is a reminder and acknowledgment that everything comes from him. We recognize that, and we respond by giving back a portion. This principle is for us, just as it was for them.

Nehemiah 9:32 says that the people placed themselves under obligation to contribute one-third of a shekel yearly for the service of the house of God. They also pledged to bring a supply of wood for the priests, so that the fire would continue to burn in the house of God. This was above and beyond their tithes and offerings. This was voluntary. This reminds me of what Jesus said, *"For I say to you, that unless your righteousness exceeds that of the Pharisees, you will not enter the kingdom of God" (Matt. 5:20).*

This new vow went beyond the first vow. This new vow included a dedication to hearing and responding to the word of God, to resting in Christ, and to surrendering their lives to God. This is a vow we as Christians can make. And when we do, we put God in a position where he can accomplish in us and through us what we in ourselves cannot accomplish.

THE CITY RESTORED

Finally, in Nehemiah 11:1, 2 we read,

Now the leaders of the people lived in Jerusalem, but the rest of the people cast lots to bring one out of ten to live in Jerusalem, the holy city, while nine-tenths remained in the other cities. And the people blessed all the men who volunteered to live in Jerusalem.

Together, Ezra and Nehemiah present the complete history of recovery. God wants to restore not only the temple (worship) and the wall (separation from the world and unity), but he also wants to populate the city.

A city is a place of government where people interact with one another under a common set of laws or rules. God wanted to bring more people into his city, to be under his government, and to live together under his sovereign rule. Practically speaking, this brings in the kingdom, where God rules and reigns in the midst of his people. Living in the same place, Jerusalem, rather than living apart and looking after their own interests, they could strengthen one another, care for one another, love one another, and be built up together.

Our culture in America today is not very conducive to a rich experience of church life. As a people, we are becoming more and more independent and, as a result, isolated from one another. An Indian missionary friend of mine once commented, while standing on my porch looking down the street, "Where are all the people?" I explained to him that here in America when people get off work they normally go to their homes, get behind closed doors, and settle down in front of the television or their computers. He replied to me that in his country people use their homes as a place to sleep, but that much of their lives are lived out on the streets or in public eating meals or drinking tea with one another.

Our individuality may be good and may be a gift from God, but for God to recover what he wants, he needs a people who are willing to commit to being in relationship with one another. He needs people who will pray together, seek him together, serve together, commit to the common purpose of seeing God's house restored, and lay down their own lives for the sake

> *Our individuality may be good and may be a gift from God, but for God to recover what he wants, he needs a people who are willing to commit to being in relationship with one another.*

of building up the church. Sometimes commitments like this may require of you things like changing your address and moving closer to other like-minded believers so that you can spend more time together and have more access to one another's lives.

But for the Lord to have what he wants, this kind of sacrifice would be well worth it.

These things: worship, separation from the world, unity, and the strengthening of the corporate life of the church are what we see in the books of Ezra and Nehemiah. These books shine a great deal of light on the path that leads back to an understanding of God's purpose for the church and what he is working to accomplish in this day. The question on our side of the equation is, how badly do we want it and what are we willing to do to have it?

Chapter Eleven

FOLLOW THE LEADER
HOW EZRA INSPIRED THE PEOPLE TO REBUILD THE HOUSE OF GOD

God uses leaders. In the course of the work of rebuilding the temple, the wall, and the city, God sent leaders to his people to inspire, instruct, cast vision, and rally them until the task was complete. While leadership style and the coordination of leaders within a local church are items for discussion, the importance of leaders is not. Leaders are indispensable to any work of God.

During this period of restoration God raised up leaders like Zerubbabel, who was the recognized prince of the tribe of Judah and leader of the returning remnant; Jeshua (Joshua), the son of Jehozadak, the first high priest after the Babylonian captivity; the prophets Haggai and Zechariah; Ezra, the teacher and scribe; and Nehemiah, the cupbearer of King Artaxerxes and the appointed governor of Judea when he returned to Jerusalem to rebuild the walls and restore the city. All these leaders were given an appointed task to accomplish.

Today we need leaders. We need people who can inspire us to press on to know the Lord, and be models for us to imitate.

We need leaders whose examples will inspire us to live godly lives before the Lord. We also need special kinds of leaders with the vision, experience, and the capability to challenge and lead corporate groups of men and women into an experience of Christian community with one another.

> *Today we need leaders. We need people who can inspire us to press on to know the Lord, and be models for us to imitate.*

I remember when I taught at an international school in Italy many years ago, that there was a history teacher there everybody loved. His class was the most popular one at the school. He loved history so much, he knew his subject matter so well, and he was so enthusiastic, that when he talked about history, everyone was inspired. Even if a student didn't particularly like history, this teacher had the ability to make what seemed like a dry subject exciting. I don't doubt that many of the students who took his class were inspired to become history majors and teachers themselves.

Another person who was a great inspiration in my life was a man who raised up a church among a group of young people in a place called Isla Vista, a university town near the University of California in Santa Barbara. At that time, I was about twenty years old and following the Lord with a group of other college-age kids. This man was given to the Lord and so given to us. He passed on to us a foundational understanding of how big a Christ we have, and of God's purpose for the church that continues to be a deep well that I've drawn from through the years. I'll never forget the time and energy he willingly gave us—how he held back nothing so that we could know and experience Jesus Christ in a profound way.

We all need examples like this. And once we've had the privilege of knowing leaders like these, we need to become examples ourselves, for others to see and emulate.

THE EXAMPLE EZRA LIFTED UP FOR THE PEOPLE TO SEE

As we've already seen, when the Lord stirred up the spirits of the remnant to return to rebuild the house of God upon its original foundations, the people began well. They finished the altar and the foundation, and all the people sang and rejoiced. They were off to such a good start. But then they got discouraged.

The enemies in the land came to them and frustrated and discouraged them and the work stopped. They were afraid to continue with this great work, so they turned away from the building of God and began focusing on building their own houses. Then God sent Haggai and Zechariah, who cast before the people a heavenly vision—pointing them to Christ, and they returned to work and completed the temple.

By the time Ezra returned to Jerusalem it was close to sixty years after the temple had been completed. But the people and the city were still in a weakened state. There was no wall; the city was barely populated; there were problems; they were still being attacked; they were pursing their own interests, and the world had become a major distraction. When Ezra returned and saw the situation, he knew that the people needed courage and inspiration. So what did he do?

As mentioned earlier, Ezra wrote not only the book of Ezra but possibly some portions of Nehemiah as well. He also wrote the book of Esther, and I and II Chronicles, and he put together the whole Old Testament. I Chronicles is the story of David. II Chronicles is the story of Solomon.

Interestingly, Israel already had those histories written down in the books of I and II Samuel and I and II Kings. So why did Ezra need to go back and re-write these same stories again?

It's very possible that I Chronicles was written during the time when the building of God in Jerusalem had come to a stop or just after Ezra returned. If so, Ezra must have written it in response to the question he surely spent long hours brooding over, "What can I say to the people that will inspire and motivate them to get back to work rebuilding the temple of God and completing the work God has called them to do?"

The people had a heart for God, but they had gotten distracted and lost courage. They needed to see a role model. They needed inspiration. So Ezra looked back some 500 years to the life of David. He decided to rewrite the story of David, but this time he would draw the people's attention to the heart of their hero David and his great love for the house of God.

As we look at Ezra's account of David's life in I Chronicles, we find that it says nothing about David's youth, about his slaying the giant Goliath, about his years as a fugitive running from King Saul, or of his sin with Bathsheba. While the book of Kings tells the history of David as a man, in the book of Chronicles, Ezra writes about David's heart.

When we see David, we see a man's man. As a boy, he became an expert marksman with his slingshot, practicing out in the fields on the wolves and bears while defending his father's sheep. As a young man, he inspired the Israelites by his courage when he fought Goliath, and the people of Israel responded by fighting the Philistines.

David was a shepherd, but he was also a mighty soldier. Jonathan felt deep love for him when he saw David fighting.

He must have been a fierce fighter. When David was hiding from Saul in wilderness caves, men kept coming to join him. Most were worthless rebels, but by following David, they were inspired, made into God's mighty men, and became heroes.

Not only was he a shepherd and a soldier, but he was also a talented singer. In today's terms he was like a rock star. He inspired King Saul and others. Not only did he inspire men, but he inspired the women as well. I Samuel 18:6, 7 says,

> *It happened as they were coming, when David returned from killing the Philistine, that the women came out of all the cities of Israel, singing and dancing, to meet King Saul, with tambourines, with joy and with musical instruments. The women sang as they played, and said, "Saul has slain his thousands, And David his ten thousands."*

What was it about David that was so inspiring? What attracted people so much to follow him? It was his heart for God.

> *What was it about David that was so inspiring? What attracted people so much to follow him? It was his heart for God.*

In the book of Deuteronomy, God told the people that after they entered the Promised Land, he would choose a place where all the tribes would go to celebrate their unity and the three annual feasts he had appointed for them. But during the entire time of the Judges and the reign of King Saul, no one ever inquired of God about where that city was to be, or where God wanted to put his name and have a house in which to rest.

But look at King David. What was his first act as king? Did he throw an elaborate, magnificent party to celebrate his coronation? No. His first act as king was to go and capture Jerusalem.

Somehow, he must have known that Jerusalem was that place. He inspired his men by telling them that the first one into the city would become his captain.

And what was his second act as king? His second act as king was to get the ark (representing the presence of God) and bring it back into the city of God.

During his 40 years as king, Saul never showed an interest in the ark or in the presence of God. But David got the ark and brought it back to Jerusalem. What a heart for God, and what an inspiration! In our day we need leaders like David, whose heart's desire is to bring the presence of God back into the church of God.

With the ark back in Jerusalem, David built a palace. But before the palace was complete, he took an oath, which we read in Psalms 132: 1-5 and 13, 14:

> *Remember, O Lord, on David's behalf, all his affliction; how he swore to the Lord and vowed to the Mighty One of Jacob, "Surely I will not enter my house, nor lie on my bed; I will not give sleep to my eyes or slumber to my eyelids, until I find a place for the Lord, a dwelling place for the Mighty One of Jacob" …For the Lord has chosen Zion; he has desired it for His habitation. "This is My resting place forever; here I will dwell, for I have desired it."*

David, with his heart for God, was the first person to see that God needed a house and do something about it. In I Chronicles chapter 28 Ezra wrote that David assembled all the leaders, commanders, officials, and the mighty men, and announced to them that God would not allow him build the house of God because he was a man of war and had shed much blood, but that his son, Solomon, would build it.

God's news to David was probably very disappointing to him at first. But what did he do? Did he sulk or feel sorry for himself? Did he curse God because God would not let him have one of his greatest dreams? No! David, because of his love for God, probably said something like this, "If I can't build it, then I will do everything in my power to prepare for it. That I *can* do. I'll provide all the resources needed for the temple. If it needs gold, I'll get the gold. If it needs wood, I'll get the wood. I'll get all the provisions and I'll make all the plans."

From that point, David had victory in every battle. From all the battles he fought, the booty that he accumulated was saved for the house of God.

Interestingly, until that time, the people only had the wilderness tabernacle. No one knew what the house of God was to look like. But God had something else for David to do for the temple. He showed David the very detailed pattern for the temple, and David wrote it all down and began drawing up the plans for the building.

God showed David the pattern for the furniture, for all the utensils, for the storehouses, for the upper and inner rooms, for the courts, and all the surrounding rooms. He showed him how the priests and Levites should be divided up for the work of service. He even showed him how much each piece of the furniture for the temple should weigh—the lampstand, the table for showbread, the candlestick, and even the cherubim that spread themselves over the Ark of the Covenant. In I Chronicles 28:19, David says *"All this the Lord made me understand in writing by His hand upon me, all the details of the pattern."*

David was consumed with all the preparations for the house of God, down to the last detail.

So David not only accumulated materials and resources for the project, but he also drew up the architectural plans. God told him about the singers. He chose the choir directors. David was consumed with all the preparations for the house of God, down to the last detail.

THE COST OF THE TEMPLE

As Ezra unfolds the story of David and his heart for the house of God, he recorded in I Chronicles 22:14 that David spoke to his son Solomon saying,

> *"Now behold, with great pains I have prepared for the House of the Lord 100,000 talents of gold and 1,000,000 talents of silver, and bronze and iron beyond weight, for they are in great quantity; also timber and stone I have prepared, and you may add to them. Moreover there are many workmen with you, stone-cutters and masons of stone and carpenters, and all the men who are skillful in every kind of work. Of the gold, the silver and the bronze and the iron there is no limit. Arise and work, and may the Lord be with you."*

It is staggering to consider, in today's dollars, how much 100,000 talents of gold and 1,000,000 talents of silver would be worth. A talent was considered the full weight a man could carry. A source in one Bible dictionary I read said that a talent was equal to about 93 pounds. A talent was also equal to 3,000 shekels. A shekel weighed approximately 11.4 grams.

Using today's dollars, the value of gold (24K) is at a current high of about $700 per ounce. According to a friend of mine in the jewelry business, there are 31.1 grams in an ounce. That means one gram would be worth about $22.50. A shekel would worth $256.50 (22.50 X 11.4). And a talent would be worth $769,500 (256.50 X 3000).

David raised 100,000 talents of gold. In today's dollars, that would have a value of $77 billion dollars!

He also raised 1,000,000 talents of silver and bronze. Assuming the cost of silver to be $10 per ounce, and using the same formula, a gram of silver would be equal to 32 cents, and a shekel of silver would be worth $3.64. One million talents of silver would be equivalent to another $11 billion dollars. So in round numbers, the monetary value of the resources David gave for the house of God would be somewhere around $88 billion dollars. And that doesn't even take into account the value of the copper and iron that were "beyond weight!"

As if all that was not enough, there is more. In the last scene of David's life that Ezra recorded for us in I Chronicles he wrote,

> *Then King David said to the entire assembly, "My son Solomon, whom alone God has chosen, is still young and inexperienced and the work is great; for the temple is not for man, but for the Lord God. Now with all my ability I have provided for the house of my God the gold for the things of gold, and the silver for the things of silver, and the bronze for the things of bronze, the iron for the things of iron, and wood for the things of wood, onyx stones and inlaid stones, stones of antimony and stones of various colors, and all kinds of precious stones and alabaster in abundance. Moreover, in my delight in the house of my God, the treasure I have of gold and silver, I give to the house of my God, **over and above all that I have already provided for the holy temple, namely, 3,000 talents of gold, of the gold of Ophir, and 7,000 talents of refined silver, to overlay the walls of the buildings...**"*
>
> (I Chron. 29:1-4) [Emphasis mine]

Not only did all the gold and silver and treasure from all of his spoils of war go into building the house of God, but with one final gesture, David reached into his own personal treasury and gave an additional 3,000 talents of

> *Truly David gave not only his whole heart and soul, but also all he had to see the Lord's house built.*

gold and 7,000 talents of silver to help beautify the house of God even more. What was that worth? In today's dollars, that was worth over one billion dollars. Truly David gave not only his whole heart and soul, but also all he had to see the Lord's house built.

What was the response to this lavish giving? In I Chronicles 29:5 Ezra quotes David as saying, *"Who then is willing to consecrate himself this day to the Lord?"*

The response was:

> *Then the rulers of the fathers' households, and the princes of the tribes of Israel, and the commanders of thousands and of hundreds, with the overseers over the king's work, offered willingly; and for the service for the house of God they gave 5,000 talents and 10,000 darics of gold, and 10,000 talents of silver, and 18,000 talents of brass, and 100,000 talents of iron. Whoever possessed precious stones gave them to the treasury of the house of the Lord, in care of Jehiel the Gershonite. Then the people rejoiced because they had offered so willingly, for they made their offering to the Lord with a whole heart; and King David also rejoiced greatly.*
>
> (I Chron. 29:6-9)

David inspired the rest of the leaders to go home and bring back their own treasures for the building. The blessing of God came down. The Lord touched the hearts of all the people. They ate and drank with great gladness. This was one of the happiest days ever recorded in the history of Israel.

When the people of Ezra's day heard this story about giving to the Lord's temple, they must have been inspired as well. They knew what they had to do. They had to give their hearts and all that they had to rebuild the house of God.

The story of David's life is truly inspiring, but David's impressive attributes and passion for the house of God were only pictures of the characteristics that would be manifest in the King of all Kings. Who inspires our hearts? Jesus. He is our inspiration. He gave everything for us, his church. When we see Jesus, again and again, we are inspired and the work of God in our lives can go forward. And as we become more like Jesus, as we grow to love what he loves, our hearts are moved to give ourselves for what he gave himself for—the church. Consider the following Scripture passages:

> ...let us run with endurance the race that is set before us, looking unto Jesus, the author and finisher of our faith, who for the joy that was set before Him [his bride, the church] endured the cross, despising the shame...
>
> (Hebrews 12: 1,2)

> "Again, the kingdom of heaven is like a merchant [Christ] seeking fine pearls, and upon finding one pearl of great value [the church], he went and sold all that he had and bought it."
>
> (Matt. 13:45, 46)

> Husbands, love your wives, just as Christ also loved the church and gave Himself up for her... "For this reason a man shall leave his father and mother and shall be joined to his wife, and the two

shall become one flesh. This mystery is great; but I am speaking with reference to Christ and the church."

(Eph. 5:25, 31, 32)

God is looking for men and women whose hearts are totally for him. If your heart is totally for God, then you will inspire others. God's purpose has neither changed nor wavered. He is in the business of building his church, of restoring the house of God, of separating his people from the world, of building them up together in love and unity as a testimony that the world might know that the Father sent the Son, and of extending the reach of his kingdom into all the earth.

> *God is looking for men and women whose hearts are totally for him. If your heart is totally for God, then you will inspire others.*

This is what God is doing today. This is his call. As in the days when King Cyrus issued his invitation to all the people to return to Jerusalem, will you be one of those who responds to his call to rebuild?

Chapter Twelve

SEEING CHRIST—THE REMEDY FOR DEAD RITUALS, DEAD RELATIONSHIPS, AND DEAD RESOURCES
THE BOOK OF MALACHI—A FINAL WORD TO THE REMNANT

There's one final book that falls within the time frame of the other books we've been looking at dealing with the remnant and the rebuilding of the house of God. That's the book of Malachi—the last book in the Old Testament.

Malachi means *the Messenger*. Nothing really substantial is known about Malachi. According to the Jewish Taragam, an Aramaic translation of the Hebrew Bible written more than a thousand years ago, the authorship of the book of Malachi was also attributed to Ezra, but there's no evidence to support that claim. Without dispute though, we know Malachi was also written to the remnant that had returned to Jerusalem, most likely during the time when Nehemiah was ministering in Jerusalem, or while he was away (probably between the years 444-415). When we add Malachi's message to what we have seen thus far, we see the final word to the remnant God had called to restore the temple, the wall, and the city.

In considering the spiritual influence of this final prophet upon the remnant, we must see that it is God's way to use a variety of servants to speak into the lives of his people.

In the days of the early church when Paul wrote to the Corinthians, he admonished them against dividing from one another based on their preference of one leader over another:

> *Now I exhort you, brethren, by the name of our Lord Jesus Christ, that you all agree and that there be no divisions among you, but that you be made complete in the same mind and in the same judgment. For I have been informed concerning you, my brethren, by Chloe's people, that there are quarrels among you. Now I mean this, that each one of you is saying, "I am of Paul," and "I of Apollos," and "I of Cephas," and "I of Christ." Has Christ been divided...For when one says, "I am of Paul," and another, "I am of Apollos," are you not mere men? What then is Apollos? And what is Paul? Servants through whom you believed, even as the Lord gave to each one. I planted, Apollos watered, but God was causing the growth.*
>
> (I Cor.1: 10-13, I Cor. 3:4-6)

Peter was an evangelist. When he came to town, some in the church eagerly anticipated the miraculous—the signs, the wonders, the supernatural. When Apollos came, there were others who were captivated by his eloquent words and teaching. As Paul said, *"For indeed Jews ask for signs and Greeks search for wisdom" (I Cor. 1:22)*. In Corinth, as today, people had their natural preferences. But that was no reason for division.

Though both Peter and Apollos were God's gifts to the body of Christ in Corinth, a steady diet of either one of them would have resulted in imbalance and immaturity in the church. Too much influence on signs and wonders can result in people minimizing the importance of teaching or study. Likewise, those who place too much emphasis on knowledge and teaching often tend to be closed to becoming involved in evangelism or the supernatural.

Looking at it on one level, we should loath division in the body of Christ because it separates us from other Christians and leaves a poor testimony for the world to see. But looking at it from a higher elevation, division robs people of the benefit of receiving from all the gifted leaders that God sends to the church. God sent Paul. God sent Apollos. And God sent Peter—all three—*for their growth!* In order to bring the brothers and sisters in Corinth to maturity in Christ, they needed to benefit from *all* that these gifted leaders had to offer.

Many years ago I learned the lesson that a church growing up primarily under the influence of one dominant leader—no matter how good or how gifted that leader is—will end up out of balance. It can't be avoided. It's like a tree in the forest that grows up leaning in one direction. The longer a church is under the influence of one leader, the more noticeable that lean will become.

> *Many years ago I learned the lesson that a church growing up primarily under the influence of one dominant leader—no matter how good or how gifted that leader is—will end up out of balance. It can't be avoided.*

A healthy church benefits from receiving a variety of leaders who minister Christ in an assortment of ways. Any leader who stays at a church for a long time will not only deposit what they minister but also who they are. If a leader has a strong personality with a bent toward being highly organizational and systematic, those traits will eventually take root in the life and practice of the church.

Similarly, a leader with an overriding flair for being spontaneous and creative will eventually manifest those characteristics
in the church as well. This can foster in a group of people the
mindset that to be spontaneous is to be spiritual (the reverse
can also occur, that to plan and be very organized is to be spiritual), when these characteristics are merely the expression of the
personality traits of those leaders.

Churches we read about in the New Testament grew under
the influence of numerous itinerant Christian workers in con-
cert with a plurality of local leaders. The itinerant workers came
to town for a period, ministered, then moved on. Sometimes
they returned, but they never stayed to take up the position we
see so often in the church today, that of a "career pastor." Each
had a timely word for God's people and delivered it in his own
unique style and personality. In this scenario, God's people
had not one leader to emulate and model their lives after, but
rather a handful.

This is God's way. Beware of a church that has no plurality of
leadership. Beware of a church where outside speakers who have
something of Christ to minister are not encouraged to come.
These situations will ultimately stifle the growth of the church
and result in a roadblock for any group of people wanting to
pursue the way of recovery and restoration.

The Old Testament remnant benefited from the varied ministries of an assortment of strong, godly leaders—Zerubbabel,
Jeshua, Haggai, Zechariah, Ezra, and Nehemiah. But there was
one more, the final prophet—the messenger Malachi—who had
his own unique contribution to make. God raised Malachi up at
the right time to address what the people still lacked, including
giving them a view of Christ that other leaders had not given
them before.

As we begin to look at the book of Malachi I want to reiterate that along with the other books of Ezra, Nehemiah, Haggai, and Zechariah, the message in this book was not for those who had decided to remain in Babylon. It was not written to a group of people who had no heart for God.

The recipients of this message were those who had returned and had responded to the call of God. They were ones who had made spiritual progress, and who had a history and a testimony of God working in their lives. These were the people (or at least their first-generation descendants) who had restored worship, won past battles, taken a stand against the world, seen God's enemies silenced and beaten back, experienced real advancement in the growth and development of the city, and seen God's government expand within it.

These were not rookies or new enlistees. They were experienced, seasoned, battle-tested veterans. But they had a problem. They had grown weary. They had become lax and as a result, had begun to compromise. They had grown tired of waiting for the promise that the Messiah would come and had lost their zeal. Once again they had begun to doubt God's love, and their commitment to him began to wane. They needed another wake-up call. So God sent his messenger Malachi.

Malachi began his book with a reminder of God's love for his people. God had loved Jacob and hated Esau. Though God's choice favored Jacob, the first few verses of Malachi call attention to Esau's inheritance, not Jacob's. The writer began with how Esau's mountains were made desolate. What it doesn't say though, and what should have been obvious to the remnant, was that it was through Jacob that Israel was given the beautiful land of Canaan as their inheritance, a land flowing with milk and honey.

The people had forgotten, or taken for granted, how beautiful their land really was in much the same way that we as Christians, after following the Lord for some time, can forget how much God loves us and lose our appreciation for the wonderful inheritance we have in the person of Jesus Christ.

DEAD RITUALS—THE PRIESTHOOD HAD BECOME DEFILED

In four short chapters, Malachi the prophet zeroed in on three areas where the people had compromised in their relationship with God: the priesthood had become defiled; marriages had been dishonored, and tithes and offerings had been forgotten. Malachi 1:7, 8 says:

> *"You are presenting defiled food upon my altar. But you say 'How have we defiled You?' "In that you say, 'The table of the Lord is to be despised.' "But when you present the blind for sacrifice, is it not evil? And when you present the lame and sick, is it not evil? Why not offer it to your governor? Would he be pleased with you? Or would he receive you kindly?" says the Lord of hosts."*

The Old Testament sacrifices and offerings were intended to be of the highest quality, because they were pictures of Christ, who is perfect and without any blemish or defect. But the priests began to compromise and offer up what was inferior. The offerings had become a form of religious obligation. What was originally presented in *life*, and with *zeal*, had degenerated into a ritual and an uninspiring, religious formality.

God's response to this disrespect was clear and direct. The people were going about their business and making their offerings but not taking it seriously, thinking that as long as they presented something to God it would be accepted even though it fell short of God's standard. But God would rather that they had hung a "gone out of business" sign on the altar and ceased making offerings altogether. In doing that, the people would have at least been more honest with God than they were being.

In Malachi 1:10 God told the people, *"Oh that there were one among you who would shut the gates that you might not uselessly kindle fire on My altar! I am not pleased with you." Says the Lord of hosts, "nor will I accept an offering from you."* God was basically saying, "Just close the gates to the city. I'm tired of people coming and making these mindless, passionless offerings to me!"

What a wake-up call, and not just for the people of Malachi's time. Like the remnant, do you sometimes become weary? Do you begin to doubt God's love for you? Has lively, heartfelt worship and love for the Lord been reduced to performing uninspiring rituals? If so, like the remnant, then you too need a wake-up call.

> *Like the remnant, do you sometimes become weary? Do you begin to doubt God's love for you? Has lively, heartfelt worship and love for the Lord been reduced to performing uninspiring rituals? If so, like the remnant, then you too need a wake-up call.*

God sees. He knows. God cares how we live our lives with him. Sometimes we think that God doesn't see when we start to slip, or when our love, admiration, and worship for him begin to wane, and we just end up going through the motions. But he does see. He's not unreasonable in what he asks.

We need to be willing to "shut the gates." We need to be willing to bring what we're doing to a halt, even if it appears to be religious or acceptable. Without life, worship and service to him are dead. Christ said to the woman at the well, *"The hour is coming, and now is, when the true worshippers will*

worship the Father in spirit and in truth [reality]" *(John 4:23).*
Our worship needs to be real. Our praise to him must not be
just warm sounding, acceptable words coming from our lips,
but originating from cold hearts.

How refreshing it is when a group of people following the
Lord together sense that their corporate worship has become
lifeless, sick, lame, and blind and are willing to shut it down
and do something different. When you come to that fork in the
road where the street sign pointing in one direction says, "The
Comfortable, Familiar, and Lifeless Way" and the sign pointing in the other direction reads, "The New, Unchartered Way,"
are you willing to choose the less frequented path and seek the
Lord, that he might do something new among you?

I have a practical example to share with you concerning a
situation like this that I experienced years ago with a group of
believers. We had just gone through the agony of a church split.
People that we thought we would spend the rest of our lives with
fellowshipping and worshiping the Lord were suddenly ripped
away from us. We had believed that we would watch our kids
grow up together, see them get married, and be there for each
another until the very end when we buried each other and celebrated our promotions to glory. But one day all of that came
to an abrupt halt and fellowship was broken. Only if you have
gone through this kind of rending ordeal yourself, or a divorce,
can you identify with the pain and turmoil it can cause.

For several years leading up to this split, our meetings together were off the charts—filled with the kind of joy, laughter,
shouting, worship, and praise that would make angels jealous.
But then came the split. Now what were we to do when we
came together? Were we to have the same kind of meetings,
and continue on as if nothing had happened? Were we to lift

our voices to shout and praise the Lord while on the inside we were grieving and dying?

Many groups do that. They continue on, season after season, doing the same things in the same way, over and over again. But could it be that God might want to use such awful situations as opportunities to stop us and point us in a new direction?

God would rather have his people be "real" as opposed to being fake or phony. If you are not feeling joyful, should you just pretend by putting on an outward façade of worship when it is not consistent with what's going on in your inner being?

In our situation, the solution was to do something that I have rarely, if ever, heard of Christians doing before. We stopped meeting. Looking back, that was probably the most practical and appropriate thing we could have done. We determined that we wouldn't meet all together as a church for six months.

What did we do in the interlude? We met together in small groups in the mornings for prayer and we continued having meals together. During those early morning prayer times there was much silence, as we just waited on the Lord together. We prayed, and we read, and we prayed the Scriptures together. But our outward expression in those small meetings was not one of exuberance. Rather, in that difficult season, it was as if we were seeking to sink our roots deeper into the Lord to find spiritual water at a deeper level.

After a few months, as we began to mend, we started to anticipate the day we would all be meeting together as a larger group again. God had used that season to bring healing and introduce us to new ways of worship that we would never have known if we had continued doing the same things we had always done before.

When we did start meeting all together the atmosphere was again one of joy, but there were new ingredients and dimensions of worship that we hadn't experienced previously. There was more depth and variety, and there were more times of silent worship, when we all humbled our hearts and quietly postured ourselves before our awesome God and waited on him. The meetings had become richer as a result of us being willing to "shut the gates" and settle for nothing less than being real with the Lord.

Our God is indeed a great God. Christ is a great King. Going through the motions of performing dead rituals does nothing for us, does nothing to impress God, and will never inspire the nations to turn to God. Passionate, sincere, and real worship toward God, in whatever form that is expressed, will always be the standard and the only thing that will sway the nations to turn to Christ. As Malachi pronounced, *"From the rising of the sun even to its setting, My name will be great among the nations"* (Malachi 1:11).

> *Going through the motions of performing dead rituals does nothing for us, does nothing to impress God, and will never inspire the nations to turn to God.*

DEAD RELATIONSHIPS—IT WAS BECOMING COMMONPLACE TO ABANDON THE COMPANION AND WIFE OF ONE'S YOUTH

At the time Malachi prophesied, the people had problems not just with dead rituals in their relationship with God but their problems extended to human relationships as well.

When Ezra had returned to Jerusalem with a burden to teach the word of God, he first had to address the problem of worldliness and confront the situation of people taking foreign wives. Nehemiah also addressed the foreign wives issue, but his main burden had been the protection of the temple worship by constructing a wall of separation.

Nehemiah was successful in motivating God's people to work together, building the wall with a trowel in one hand and fighting the battle with a sword in the other. When there was a breach in one part of the wall and the enemy attacked, the trumpet was blown and people from one section of the wall came to the aid and rescue of those under assault. So Ezra had a teaching ministry and Nehemiah's ministry was characterized by unifying and protecting the people, but how was Malachi's ministry any different?

The first issue Malachi took on was the polluted priesthood. The next was failed marriages and family relations, and finally the withholding of tithes and offerings. Malachi's messages were aimed at personal holiness. Without holiness in our relationship to God (failure of the priests), to our families (failure in marriage), and to meeting the needs of others and deploying resources for kingdom purposes (failure in the tithes and offerings), the remnant was once again stopped dead in their tracks. The church of God has the same problems today. When any group of people becomes weighed down by dead rituals, dead relationships, and dead resources, it's time once again to hear from a prophet like Malachi.

There had been so many failed marriages, divorces, and marriages or remarriages to pagan wives that the people had grown accustomed to it. They were used to these alarming things, and had come to accept them. In fact, some were probably thinking to themselves, "Others are doing it and getting away with it, why can't I?" The moral bar for acceptable behavior among the Lord's people had been lowered—a lot. But God hates divorce, not only for the pain and damage it brings to the lives of the couple involved, but also to their children, their extended families, and their friends, not to mention the poor testimony it displays to the world.

Maintaining family relationships takes work—a lot of work. For many people, even after years of walking with the Lord, it can be very difficult to keep these relationships in tact and to invest the time and effort needed in order for them to be healthy and satisfying. The challenges can get more difficult, and temptations can appear

> *Maintaining family relationships takes work—a lot of work. During the marathon of life, these relationships come under fire from every possible direction.*

more alluring. During the marathon of life, these relationships come under fire from every possible direction. Rationalization, unmet needs, unrealistic expectations, childhood wounds, and other problems will eventually come to the surface. They will either overcome us or drive us to deeper levels of learning that the Lord is enough, that he is sufficient, no matter how difficult the circumstance.

Are these things Malachi's audience faced really so different from what we face today? The people had grown weary waiting for the coming of the Lord. They had taken their eyes off of Christ. But Malachi reminded them that suddenly the Lord would appear in his temple, and that he would be as one who is like a refiner's fire and a fuller's soap.

> *"Behold, I am going to send My messenger, and he will clear the way before Me. And the Lord, whom you seek, will suddenly come to His temple; and the messenger of the covenant, in whom you delight, behold He is coming," says the Lord of hosts. "But who can endure the day of His coming? And who can stand when he appears? For He is like a refiner's fire and like a fuller's soap.*

*He will sit as a smelter and purifier of silver, and He will purify
the sons of Levi and refine them like gold and silver, so that they
may present to the Lord offerings in righteousness."*

(Malachi 3:1-3)

THE MESSENGER OF THE COVENANT

In this passage Malachi referred to Jesus as *The Messenger of
the Covenant* and revealed him as the one consumed with zeal to
purify the house of God. This is the Jesus we see in John chapter
two, who was consumed with zeal for his father's house and
violently overturned the moneychangers' tables in the temple.
This is the Jesus we also see in Revelation whose *"eyes were like
a flame of fire" (Revelation 1:7).*

The covenant Malachi referred to was the new covenant.
He prophesied of a coming day when God's people would
be released from the old covenant, consisting of the Law, and
enter into a new covenant with the Lord. When the fullness of
time finally came and Christ, the Messenger of the Covenant
appeared, this promise was fulfilled.

What Malachi looked forward to—the transition from the
old covenant and the Law, to the new covenant—the apostle
Paul looked back on, when he wrote in Galatians:

*Why the Law then? It was added because of transgressions, hav-
ing been ordained through angels by the agency of a mediator,
until the seed [Christ] would come to whom the promise had
been made. Now a mediator is not for one party only; whereas
God is only one. Is the Law then contrary to the promises of God?
May it never be! For if a law had been given which was able to
impart life, then righteousness would indeed have been based on
law. But the Scripture has shut up everyone under sin, so that
the promise by faith in Jesus Christ might be given to those who*

believe. But before faith came, we were kept in custody under the law, being shut up to the faith which was later to be revealed. Therefore the Law has become our tutor to lead us to Christ, so that we may be justified by faith. But now that faith has come, we are no longer under a tutor.

(Gal. 3:19-25)

Here Paul argued that the Law was given to reveal to us our own sinfulness in the light of God's holiness and to show us our need for Christ (verse 19). It also served to provide a protective custody for us until faith came, so we would not destroy ourselves (verse 23). And finally, the Law was our tutor to lead us to Christ so that we might be justified by faith (verse 23).

But the Law given by Moses (consisting of the 10 Commandments, and the broader laws found in the Pentateuch) did not invalidate a covenant that God made with Abraham 430 years earlier (Gal. 3:17). His covenant with Abraham, like the new covenant, was a covenant of pure grace based on what God had done. *"Abraham believed God and it was reckoned to him as righteousness. Therefore, be sure that it is those who are of faith who are sons of Abraham"* (Gal. 3:6, 7).

Paul went to great lengths in Galatians chapter three to prove to his readers from their own experience and from the Old Testament Scriptures that no one has ever been saved by obeying the Law. The Lord Jesus was the only one who could perfectly fulfill the requirements of the Law. The Law was never given to us as a means of salvation or justification. Faith has ever and always been the only means of salvation, even to those living under the Law.

There is only one Savior, Jesus—for all people, for all time. The difference between those under the old covenant and those under the new covenant is one of perspective. They were looking forward to the coming of the Savior, and we are looking back at his coming.

In the parable of the Good Shepherd in John chapter ten, Jesus announced that he was the one who would lead his people out of the sheepfold (Judaism and the Law) into the pasture (Christ himself). The sheepfold was only a temporary holding place for the sheep until the time when they could be led out into pasture. In this parable Jesus also told of other sheep (the Gentiles), that were not of this fold, that would also hear his voice, and together all of his sheep, become one flock with one shepherd (John 10:16).

This parable came immediately after Jesus healed a man on the Sabbath day who had been blind from birth (John chapter nine). When this formerly blind man was brought to the Pharisees, they grilled him about who had opened his eyes. His interrogators went so far as to accuse Jesus of being a sinner. The man responded by saying, *"Whether He is a sinner, I do not know; one thing I do know, that though I was blind, now I see"* *(John 9:25).*

In this debate, this formerly blind, new convert got the best of the Pharisees. Displaying a wisdom they could not match, he went on to say that, *"Since the beginning of time it has never been heard that anyone opened the eyes of a person born blind. If this man were not from God, He could do nothing" (John 9:32-33).* As is the case with so many who receive Christ in the hostile environment of religion, be it Islam, radical Hinduism, Judaism, or even in the congregations of some nominal Christian churches, this man was forced to pay a costly price for his testimony. He was expelled. The Pharisees told him, *"You were born entirely in sins, and are you teaching us? So they put him out"* [Out from the synagogue] *(John 9:34).*

A surface reading of this story indicates that it was the Jews who cast him out, but actually it was Jesus who had opened the door for him and led him out of the sheepfold. This man was no longer confined by the fold of Judaism. He was destined to become a follower of the true shepherd of the sheep.

Malachi foretold that when the Messenger of the Covenant would come it would bring great joy. *"But for you who fear my name, the sun of righteousness will rise with healing in its wings; and you will go forth and skip about like calves from the stall"* *(Mal. 4:2).* When Christ would come, God's people would be released from being under the custody of the Law and they would know real freedom.

"You shall know the truth and the truth shall set you free."
(John 9:32)

"If the Son makes you free, you will be free indeed."
(John 9:36)

Malachi 4:2 said that they would skip like calves. They would be released from the Law into a new covenant with God, characterized by knowing a God who lived within as the life-giving Spirit, and the earmark of that new relationship would be freedom. Similarly, the apostle Paul presented the same truth to the Corinthians when he wrote, *"Now the Lord is the Spirit, and where the Spirit of the Lord is, there is liberty"* *(II Corinthians 3:17).*

> *They would be released from the Law into a new covenant with God, characterized by knowing a God who lived within as the life-giving Spirit, and the earmark of that new relationship would be freedom.*

DEAD RESOURCES—BLESSINGS WITHHELD FROM GOD'S PEOPLE AND THE NATIONS

Malachi not only took on dead rituals and dead relationships, but also dead resources. This lack of a giving heart was represented by their withholding their tithes and offerings.

> *"For I, the Lord, do not change; therefore you, O sons of Jacob, are not consumed. From the days of your fathers you have turned aside from My statutes and have not kept them. Return to Me, and I will return to you," says the Lord of hosts. "But you say, 'How shall we return?' "Will a man rob God? Yet you are robbing Me! But you say, 'How have we robbed You?' In tithes and offerings. "You are cursed with a curse, for you are robbing Me, the whole nation of you! Bring the whole tithe into the storehouse, so that there may be food in My house, and test Me now in this," says the Lord of hosts, "if I will not open for you the windows of heaven and pour out for you a blessing until it overflows. Then I will rebuke the devourer for you, so that it will not destroy the fruits of the ground nor will your vine in the field cast its grapes," says the Lord of hosts. All nations will call you blessed for you shall be a delightful land," says the Lord of hosts."*
>
> (Malachi 3:6-12)

The people were clearly disobeying what was right to do regarding tithes and offerings. The Law was specific when it came to these things. They knew what to do, and should have done it, both because it was prescribed under the Law, and because they loved God and wanted to please him and to provide resources to promote those things that God wanted promoted.

But when people begin questioning the Lord's love and start drifting spiritually, they can become more centered on themselves than others, and giving to God's purposes can suffer greatly. As we've already seen from Barna's research, the typical adult, American, churched, born-again Christian gives away only three percent of their income each year. In a world where half the population lives on only two dollars a day, even those who consider themselves to be poor or middle class here in the USA are fabulously rich compared to those living in poorer, less evangelized countries. God has blessed America beyond measure materially. An estimated 90% of all Christian philanthropy comes from the West. But an interesting footnote to this statistic is that about 80-90% of all Christian giving originating in the USA stays in the USA. That means relatively little is used to fuel worldwide missionary efforts and help the poor in less fortunate countries around the world.

Of the amount that stays in the USA, what is money used for? Things like paying mortgages on multi-million dollar church buildings, paving parking lots, building multi-purpose complexes for youth programs, and keeping the professional clergy system alive. Yet with all this money changing hands, what has this done to produce a vibrant church in America? Let's be honest and look once again at Barna's statistics: eight out of ten believers do not feel they have entered into the presence of God during the typical worship service; most people will never lead even one person to Christ and do not have specific people in mind for whose salvation they are praying, and 85% of men do not like going to church. The indicators are not good.

Most people tense up when they sit in church and hear the pastor begin to wind up and deliver that old, familiar message about how it's our duty as Christians to tithe and give our 10% to God. Still, it usually succeeds in triggering a knee-jerk reaction, and people respond to that message by reaching in their pockets and throwing something in the offering plate to appease their conscience and do their Christian duty. But this couldn't be further from what God wants our attitude to be toward managing our resources and giving for the benefit of kingdom purposes.

Many Christians are still confused about whether or not the old covenant that God made with the physical race of Jewish people, which involved the Law, has any application to us today in regard to the tithe. The deeper question that needs to be examined is, with the coming of the new covenant, are there now two covenants or only one? Is the old covenant still valid for us, and if so are we still under parts of the Law, or all of it? Or, if we are under only parts of the Law, how do we know which parts apply? Or, are we free from the Law entirely?

Can we really trust what the book of Hebrews tells us where it says that when the new covenant came, the old became obsolete (Heb. 8:13)? Can we rely upon what the apostle Paul wrote in the following passages?

But if you are led by the Spirit, you are not under the Law.
(Gal. 5:18)

"For through the Law I died to the Law, so that I might live to God."
(Gal. 2:19)

Therefore, my brethren, you were also made to die to the Law through the body of Christ, so that you might be joined to another, to Him who was raised from the dead, in order that we might bear fruit for God....But now we have been released from the Law, having died to that by which we were bound, so that we serve in newness of the Spirit and not in oldness of the letter.
(Rom. 7:4, 6)

One of the most obvious places where this question is put to the test concerning whether or not we are living under one covenant or two is in this matter of the tithe. The tithe was clearly part of the old covenant. So the question is, how does the New Testament deal with this matter of tithing? Are Christians obligated to tithe?

The New Testament contains no specific verses saying that "Christians should all tithe," or "Christians should not tithe." So we must look deeper. Consider the frequency with which the word "tithing" occurs in the New Testament. It's used eight times. Jesus gave one teaching on tithing that is recorded in Matthew, Mark, and again in Luke. In the passage in Luke he said, *"But woe to you Pharisees! For you pay tithe of mint and rue and every kind of garden herb, and yet disregard justice and the love of God; but these are the things you should have done without neglecting the others" (Luke 11:42).* But Jesus was speaking to those living under the old covenant. The new covenant had not yet been inaugurated, so these passages referring to tithing are not applicable here. That uses up three times the word is mentioned, so now we're down to five. The other five times the word is used in the New Testament are found in the book of Hebrews (chapter seven) in the context of a discussion about Melchizedek.

When you look at Paul's writings, you find that he never taught tithing! Under the new covenant we're never told what percentage of our income we have to give to the Lord. Yet isn't it interesting how much the word "tithing" is still used in Christian vocabulary today? The predominant New Testament passages that do deal with Christian giving (I Cor. 16:1 and 2, II

When you look at Paul's writings, you find that he never taught tithing!

Cor. chapters eight and nine, and Phil. chapter four) never mention the word "tithe" at all. These passages give us the following understanding of what it means to be under the new covenant in relation to the stewardship of our resources:

1. Give regularly.
2. Give joyfully as the Lord prospers you.
3. Give in relation to what you purpose in your heart to give.
4. And in some cases, give sacrificially.

That's it! Giving should be a result of your personal relationship with Christ, where you become a responder and act according to what he is directing you to do with your resources. Giving should not be guilt driven. If you can't give with joy, don't give! Most people who try to meet that bar of 10% fail miserably anyway. Just ask Barna.

If God puts on your heart to give 10% of your net or gross income, great! But what if you happen to be rich? Should you be limited to giving 10% when you need far less to meet your basic needs and your surplus could help other people or be put to use in ways that would significantly advance the gospel? No! If we will listen, God will speak to our hearts, and out of that speaking and that relationship with Christ, we can purpose in our hearts what to give, where to give, and how often to give. This attitude should characterize a new covenant Christian, and should distinguish a corporate group of believers seeking to restore the house of God on its original foundation.

What confusion reigns when people believe both covenants are still operative and apply to us as Christians! We were not intended to be straddling them both, with one foot planted in one and one planted in the other. If, as a Christian, you believe that all Christians should tithe, then what do you believe when it comes to ordering from a seafood menu at a nice restaurant? Would you have the liberty to partake of a succulent lobster tail or Alaskan king crab leg dipped in warm butter and lemon juice? Or what about eating a slice of ham at a holiday party? Or chomping on a few links of country sausage with your eggs at breakfast? Or enjoying a hot dog at a sporting event? Is eating things like shellfish or pork "off the table" for a Christian? It should be if you adhere to the Law.

Was Paul misleading us when he wrote concerning food in Romans 14:20, that "all things are clean?" If you believe that we must tithe (part of the Law), how can you then turn around and also eat the things you like to eat that go against the Law? Which is it? One covenant or two? And if you say that we are only under parts of the Law and not others, how do you decide which ones we are under and which we are not under?

What freedom we have in Christ! How liberating it is to follow the indwelling Spirit for guidance, whether it pertains to eating or giving! What a blessing it is to have resources because as we allow Christ to direct how we should use those resources, doors can open to countless possibilities to see the kingdom of God expand and the life of God flow into and through other people's lives!

Ultimately, we're not here on this earth to acquire things, but to worship God. Part of that worship includes putting our finances under his control so that others will be blessed and brought into the kingdom.

The remnant in Malachi's day was under the Law and we are not, but some of the same, timeless principles of stewardship that applied to them, apply to us as well. The remnant had lost sight of the fact that all they had been given belonged to God and they had closed their hearts to giving. As a result,

God's hand of blessing was withheld. By remembering that all we have belongs to and comes from him, we guard ourselves against closing our hearts to giving as they did.

When we see Christ and are touched by his love, the tight grip we can have on our purse strings is loosened. Martin Luther is said to have stated that a person undergoes three conversions: one of the heart, one of the mind, and one of the pocketbook. In the area of holiness—personal or corporate—the Lord is as a refiner's fire and a fuller's soap. He will not relent from purifying his people in regard to their worship, their relationships, and their resources, until all that is left is silver and gold.

> *When we see Christ and are touched by his love, the tight grip we can have on our purse strings is loosened.*

THE BOOK OF REMEMBRANCE

Malachi had one last admonition for the weary pilgrims participating in the restoration. Sometimes in the seasons of our Christian experience we can go for days, weeks, and even as long as years being in a dry and thirsty place. And sometimes we're called upon to walk through trials with the Lord in "naked faith," having no outward, perceptible assurances or feelings of his tangible presence with us. These are the times when many people give up, quit, and ride off toward the bright lights of instant gratification.

But these are also the times when the Lord is testing us to see if we are following him because of his blessings, or because he is worthy to be followed for who he is, regardless of whether or not we are feeling or experiencing a momentary display of those blessings. Will we just believe and obey, despite the circumstances? As it says in that great faith chapter in chapter 11 of the book of Hebrews, *"Without faith it is impossible to please God (Hebrews 11:6).*

You may sometimes think that God has put you on the shelf. You may think that the choices you make to follow him don't seem to matter. You may think that he no longer sees or cares, and as a result you feel justified in going off the reservation and living life for yourself. But be assured, you are not the first to ever have those thoughts. Malachi recorded God's words for a people who were in that very same condition:

> *"Your words have been arrogant against Me," says the Lord. "Yet you say, "What have we spoken against You?" "You have said, "It is vain to serve God' and what profit is it that we have kept His charge, and that we have walked in mourning before the Lord of hosts?"*
>
> (Mal. 3:13, 14)

So, you think the Lord doesn't see? Do you think that he doesn't know your thoughts? Do you think that he doesn't know when you've given up living for him and started living as if you don't know him? Do you think you can fool him by burying and hiding those thoughts of discouragement? Do you think that you can con him

The reality is that God does see. He not only sees your discouragement and disobedience, but he sees something else. He sees your faithfulness as well.

when you have given up on him inwardly, while still going through the motions outwardly? The reality is that God does see. He not only sees your discouragement and disobedience, but he sees something else. He sees your faithfulness as well. He wants to encourage you to walk in that faithfulness because in the end, there will be great reward.

> *Then those who feared the Lord spoke to one another, and the Lord gave attention and heard, and a book of remembrance was written before him for those who fear the Lord and who esteem his name. "They will be Mine," says the Lord of hosts, "on the day that I prepare My own possession, and I will spare them as a man spares his own son who serves him."*
>
> (Malachi 3:16, 17)

Often we need to be reminded that God never stops seeing and never ceases caring. Coming down the homestretch of our journey with Christ we need to believe that our faithfulness will be rewarded. We need to remain faithful to that heavenly vision. These were the words the remnant needed to hear, and they are what we need to hear to help us through hard times and help carry us across the finish line.

THE CHALLENGE
CONCLUSION

The Spirit of God is visiting the nations. In the decade of the 1990s, revival came to countries like Russia and China. At the turn of the new millennium, after 1,300 years of bondage and darkness under Islam, we're seeing the beginnings of a new move of God among people in the Muslim world in countries like Algeria and Morocco. In 2006, satellite Christian television began broadcasting 24/7 into Iran. Thousands are now coming to Christ and house churches are popping up like popcorn, even amid persecution.

These extraordinary moves of God have been taking place in countries that had been closed or hostile to the gospel for decades or centuries. This book was primarily written to those Christians who have grown up in the West, where the church has been rooted for hundreds of years but for the most part, has lost much of its vitality.

The question that many people wrestle with is, if it is God's eternal purpose and his intense desire to see the church shining like a bright lampstand, lifting up Christ for the world to see, then why can it be such an arduous, grueling challenge to find and be a part of such a church? After all, if we are clear on what God is after, and if we've committed our hearts to him, then getting there from where we are, with his help, should be a simple, straight shot, right? Maybe a few bends and turns in the road, but since we have the roadmap, possibly in a few weeks, or months, or even a year, we should be having the kind of church experience that God has always wanted for us to have, right?

Unfortunately it doesn't always work out that way. I've known of small groups of people who have waited for years, faithfully praying for God to move and to rebuild his house in their cities. Many are still waiting and have become intercessors.

Praise God, however, for the current move of his Spirit we are beginning to see in this country. Praise God that he continues to touch people's lives. Praise God for the revolutionaries Barna has identified who are not satisfied with the status quo and are doing something about it. Praise God for those who are seeking, questioning, and leaving the captivity of dead institutions in search of something more.

But the question needs to be raised: where is this search for something more leading people? As I pointed out at the beginning of this book, Barna's findings indicate that if you love the Lord and are searching for something more, and you do take that step to leave the traditional church, you will probably find yourself pursuing some form of house church, "cyber-church," or the family unit, as the place to invest your efforts to find more fulfillment in the Christian experience.

All of these things can play a part in the recovery of what God wants to bring about among his people, but do any of them, by themselves, fully restore the church to its original intention? We've looked at what God wanted to do in restoring his people from their captivity in the Old Testament. All of this was a picture for us, a roadmap as it were, for how we might look to the Lord and the Scriptures for guidance out of the current fallen situation of Christianity today and reunite with the heart and eternal purpose of God to restore the church to what he has always intended for it to be.

Though there is the aspect of the church that is universal—comprising all the members of the body of Christ—we see clearly throughout the New Testament writings, and especially from the first chapter of Revelation, that the church is also local. God saw a lampstand in each of the seven cities of Asia to whom this letter containing the Revelation was sent. He saw a lampstand in Ephesus, in Smyrna, in Pergamum, in Thyatira, in Sardis, in Philadelphia, and in Laodicea.

So the restoration of the church has a very practical and local application. God wants to have a bright, shining lampstand where Christ is exalted in every place. In order to have that, we need to seek God and make ourselves available to him to use us to help restore local expressions of the church where:

- People are resting in him and trusting in his provision.
- There is an understanding of the finished work of Christ on the cross.
- There is real, corporate worship.
- There is true Christian fellowship and unity based on knowing Christ together with other believers in a corporate setting.
- People understand and practice what it means to go to the cross and die to self.
- People understand the nature of spiritual warfare.
- Christian workers have been raised up who can give people a vision of Christ.

- The proper understanding and practice of spiritual authority within the body of Christ is practiced.
- God's government and rule are being manifest.
- There is an environment, particularly in meetings, where all members can participate and build one another up through the proper exercising of their spiritual gifts.
- The priesthood of all believers is practiced.
- There is an understanding and experience of what it means to live *in Christ* and walk by the Spirit.
- Brothers and sisters in Christ can fight their spiritual battles together.
- There is a heart for the lost.
- People are hearing the Word of God for themselves.
- People are free from the old covenant and have fully embraced the new covenant, which Christ brought about by shedding his own blood.
- Generosity and love abound.
- Holiness and a zeal for the things of God are found.
- People remain faithful to the heavenly vision.
- Having done all, believers continue to stand.

To have all these things goes well beyond just having an independent house church or home group meeting with some other believers. It goes well beyond networking, chat rooms, downloading messages, and relating to other believers over the Internet. And it even goes well beyond just raising our children in a godly manner and placing all of our energies on the family unit.

It's seeing God restore the church to what it ought to be, *in your location; in the place in which you live!* This is a challenge! This is a high calling. It may even seem like an impossible calling, but should that be surprising? If you'll remember, that's the same way the remnant felt when they were faced with re-building the temple in their day. To go this route, *it will take a commitment by a group of people to Christ and to others with a common vision.* And it will take time. But who ever said it was going to be easy?

There are no pat and easy answers for those desiring to see and be a part of the restoration of God's house and want to know: How do we start? Where do we go? What do we do? Who can help us? How can we (or I) find others in my location with the same heart?

The most solid recommendation I can give you would be that if anything in this book has touched or challenged you, begin by bringing those things to the Lord in prayer and ask him to make them real in your life. You may also want to ask yourself, "Are there others I know that I could share and discuss this book with who may also be interested in praying and seeking the Lord together about these things?"

Beyond that, be assured that there are many others out there who are asking the same questions. You can find a growing number of websites nowadays dedicated to networking and linking like-minded Christians together who have a heart for the house of God and the things discussed in this book. Some even have directories where you can find other believers with similar interests in your area. If you'd like, you can visit my website at www.TheRevelation.com and find links to these and other sites with helpful resources.

God is sovereign. He has always been the initiator. He is the one who will prepare and raise up the "Zerubbabels" of today whom he will use to guide and lead others in the way of restoration. He is also the one who will gather the people and form the new wineskins that will contain the new wine he wants to pour out when old structures have become too rigid and hardened (Mark 2: 21,22).

So from beginning to end, the work of restoration is God's work. But as we have seen, it is also a work that not all of God's people will choose to be part of. Throughout the generations, he

> *So from beginning to end, the work of restoration is God's work.*

has had his remnant. In the end, he will get all the glory. God's work begins, continues, and will find its completion as Christ is exalted, revealed, and made manifest. He is the head of his church, which is his body.

The challenge, therefore, remains for the remnant of this generation. Are you one of those who see the condition of the church today in much the same way as the people of God in the Babylonian captivity saw the house of God in Jerusalem lying in waste more than 2,500 years ago? Are you one of those willing to do something about it?

God has given us the story of Ezra and the other books of the Bible concerning the returning remnant to encourage us and to show us the way back. May those of you who have read this book not only hear the call to rebuild as loudly and as clearly as they did in the days when Cyrus issued his proclamation and invitation, but may you be like those whose spirits were stirred up and join with others to act in response to that call.

> *"Whoever there is among you of all His people, may his God be with him! Let him go up to Jerusalem which is in Judah and rebuild the house of the Lord, the God of Israel."*